Dragonfly Card
by Robin Knutson
See pages 4 - 9 for more information on Alcohol Inks

This unique coloring technique by Tim Holtz produces an unusual swirl of colors and a metallic print.

*"**Monoprint:** A one-of-a-kind print with different designs or textures."*

SIZE: 5" x 5¾"

MATERIALS: *Ranger Adirondack* Alcohol Inks - Denim, Cranberry, Pesto, Lettuce • Jet Black *Archival* Ink • Copper *Metallic Mixatives* • Blending Solution • *Gloss Paper* • *Inkssentials Non-Stick Craft Sheet*

SUPPLIES: Foam stamp (*Plaid* Elegant Dragonfly) • Ochre pattern paper • ¾" hoop earring • 12" of ½" wide ribbon • 5¾" x 10" of Rust cardstock

INSTRUCTIONS:
Monoprint: See page 7 for "Monoprint" instructions. 1. Squiggle Copper Metallic Mixatives onto Craft Sheet. Add 2 to 5 colors of Adirondack Alcohol Inks lines, dots, etc. directly over the Metallic Mixatives Ink to create color variations for a Monoprint Background. • 2. Apply a squiggle of Blending Solution. This further mixes together the colors. • 3. Place a piece of gloss cardstock GLOSS side down over the colors. • 4. Press and twist in ONE direction. Smoosh and lift to transfer colors to the cardstock. Allow to dry. • 5. Stamp a foam Dragonfly stamp on top with Archival Ink. Allow to dry.

Card: 6. Cut pattern paper to 5½" x 4¾". Adhere to front of card. • 7. Cut "Monoprint" to 4" x 4". Adhere to pattern paper. • 8. Add beads to hoop earring and attach with the ribbon.

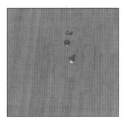

1. Dot *Metallic Mixatives* onto a craft sheet.

2. Squiggle *Alcohol Ink* over *Metallic Mixative.*

3. Add drops of *Blending Solution* into the mixture.

4. ... ove... Smoosh card. Repeat as desired.

Ink Essentials 3

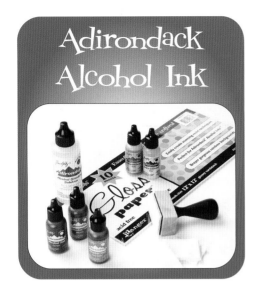

Adirondack
Alcohol Ink

Adirondack Inked 'Madison' Scrapbook Page
by Robin Beam

With Adirondack Alcohol Inks an entire scrapbook page can be created. Go from Black and White or clear plastic, metal and paper to wonderful color.

Did you notice? Not one stamp was used in this page.

SIZE: 12" x 12"

MATERIALS: *Ranger Adirondack*: Alcohol Ink Applicator; Replacement Felt; Alcohol Blending Solution; Alcohol Inks - Eggplant, Wild Plum, Denim, Stonewashed, Butterscotch, Lettuce, Meadow, Terra Cotta, Red Pepper, Stream; *Metallic Mixatives* - Silver, Pearl • *Inkssentials Non-Stick Craft Sheet* • *Cleansit* Stamp Cleaner • *Gloss Paper* - 12" x 12" White, Black" • *Glossy Accents* • *Popit! Shapes* ⅛" Squares

SUPPLIES: *American Crafts* White Sans Capital Metalgram Letters • *Magic Scraps* Blank Freeze Frames • *Junkitz -Tim Holtz* (Clearz No Hole Tabz, Round Mosaicz; Silver Metalz Snapz; Black Epoxy Stickerz: Family-Friends, Expressions) • Glue stick • Photos

Color Metal Letters with Alcohol Inks

Colorized Metal Snapz

Alcohol Agate Background on 12" x 12" Gloss Paper

Colorized Plastic

Color Metal Letters with Metallic Mixatives

Custom Epoxy Stickers

INSTRUCTIONS:

Create Gradated Alcohol Agate Scrapbook Paper:

1. The paper is a progression of color from Dark Purple to Light Blue. For the top portion of the paper, apply a squeeze of Wild Plum and Eggplant on the Ink Applicator. Add a squeeze of Blending Solution to the felt. This will help blend the colors and will allow them to go further. • 2. Tap the Ink Applicator to the top portion of the Gloss side of the scrapbook page. Twist and turn the Applicator handle to get a variegated coverage of ink. • 3. Remove the felt and place a new piece on the Velcro. • 4. Add Eggplant, Denim and Stonewashed Alcohol Inks and repeat the process with the next ⅓ of the page. 5. Again replace the handle with clean felt. This is done so that each application will be a fresh color and will not be muddy.

6. For the bottom third of the page use Denim and Stonewashed. Toward the bottom add more Blending Solution, but not additional ink so that it will be the lightest shade of Blue. • 7. To create additional "texture" to the page shake on dots of color onto the page

from the bottle. (Shake as if shaking hot sauce!) You will see how the Alcohol Ink will almost "part" from the ink you had on the page, creating bursts of color. • 8. Repeat step 7 with the Blending Solution. Put aside.

To Create the Band of Pearly Color for the Title:

9. Cut out a 3" wide strip of Black Gloss cardstock.

10. Thoroughly shake up Pearl Metallic Mixatives. You want to hear the mixing ball moving in the bottle. Add a small squeeze of Pearl on clean felt on the Ink Applicator. Add a dot of Denim and Stonewashed Alcohol Ink. • 11. Tap color onto the Black Gloss paper. Metallic Mixatives are metallic and pearl alcohol ink that blend with the alcohol inks and Blending Solution. On Dark or Black gloss cardstock, the Alcohol Ink will mix with the Pearl and colorize it. You can then see the subtle color with the Pearl on the paper. Set aside. • 12. Colorizing Metal: Spell out chosen word. Check placement of the letters before coloring them to be sure it will fit on the page. • 13. Thoroughly shake Silver Metallic Mixatives and squeeze a small amount on a clean piece of felt on the Ink Applicator. • 14. Color the letter "M". Allow the first coat to

dry (this won't take long) and apply second coat until you have opaque coverage on the letter. On a clean piece of felt, add Denim and Stonewashed Alcohol Ink. Color the letters with a coat of ink. Allow to dry. • 15. Apply a second layer of ink on the letters, blowing on the ink. The color will move and dry in different concentrations of color.

Colorizing Plastic Tilez, Mosaicz and Metal Snapz:
16. Choose various sizes of Tilez and Mosaicz. It's always a good idea to figure placement on the page before coloring them so just the right amount are made.
17. Color each Tilez and Mosaicz with one color of Alcohol Ink. Many times one coat is sufficient. Sometimes you will find that the Alcohol Inks "bead" on the plastic. To resolve this, clean the plastic with Blending Solution or Cleansit Stamp Cleaner to remove any coating that may have been on the plastic. • 18. For the Snapz Eggplant and Wild Plum were squeezed onto a clean piece of felt on the Ink Applicator and color tapped onto tops of the Snapz.

Creating Color Epoxy Stickerz:
19. For this page, one color of Alcohol Ink was applied to scrap White Gloss Paper.
20. Remove protective backing on the chosen Epoxyz words and adhere to the Alcohol Ink colored paper. Trim with scissors. • 21. Option: Alcohol Ink can also be applied directly to the top of the Epoxyz as was explained in Steps 18-19.

Finishing:
22. Glue pearlized strip of paper with a glue stick. Attach letters on top with Popit! Shapes cut up to fit behind the metal. • 23. Attach filmstrip transparency with small dots of Glossy Accents on the ends and in the middle of the strip. Place down and press firmly. • 24. Attach photos with glue stick. • 25. Attach Snapz, Epoxyz , Tilez and Mosaicz with Glossy Accents.

Tips and Techniques
1. Do not add more than one dot of each color of Alcohol Ink on the felt; otherwise the colors will muddy.

2. Always allow the first application of Alcohol Ink to dry before placing on the next layer; otherwise the colors will muddy.

3. Remember that you can use *Metallic Mixatives* by themselves to color and create backgrounds on non-porous surfaces and *Gloss Paper*.

4. If you want to color the entire Snapz (indented area as well as the high spots) drop some inks in a zip bag, add the Snapz and maneuver the ink and Snapz around the closed bag with your fingers. Once you have achieved the color that you want, remove from bag onto Craft Sheet and allow to dry.

5. Note: a little drop of *Glossy Accents* goes a long way, so use a small amount. When you press down the item to be attached, it will spread out.

1. Apply ink to an applicator.

2. Apply *Blending Solution* to an applicator.

3. Tap applicator onto White Gloss Paper.

4. Drip drops of ink and *Blending Solution* onto page.

5. Apply Ink to an applicator.

6. Tap ink onto Black Gloss Paper.

7. Apply *Metallic Mixative* onto an applicator.

8. Tap *Mixative* onto letter. Let Dry and repeat.

9. Apply ink onto an applicator.

10. Tap onto letter. Let dry.

11. Apply 2nd layer. Blow to move & dry in unique patterns.

12. Clean Tilez with *Blending Solution*.

13. Apply ink onto an applicator.

14. Tap ink onto Tilez.

15. Apply ink to an applicator.

16. Tap ink onto Snapz.

17. Apply Ink to applicator.

18. Tap onto scrap Gloss Paper.

19. Remove Epoxyz backing & adhere to inked area.

20. Cut out Epoxyz.

Happy Flower Card
by Kate Farricker

SIZE: 5" x 7"

MATERIALS: *Ranger Adirondack* Alcohol Ink - Cranberry, Lettuce, Pesto, Slate • *Metallic Mixatives* - Gold, Copper, Pearl • Cranberry and Gold for Background; Slate and Pearl for Daisy; Pesto, Lettuce and Copper for Scallop • *Glossy Accents* • Jet Black *Archival* Ink Pad • *Gloss Paper*

SUPPLIES: Rubber stamps (*Hero Arts* Daisy Blossom, Big and Bold Happy; *Stampers Anonymous* Paper Scallop) • Ribbon • Glass Glitter

INSTRUCTIONS: **Monoprint:** See page 7 for "Monoprint" instructions. Stamp "happy" and flower. Cut out flower. Adhere glitter to center with Glossy Accents.

Flower Bouquet
by Madeline Arendt

SIZE: 5" x 7"

MATERIALS: *Ranger Adirondack*: Alcohol Ink - Red Pepper, Pesto; *Metallic Mixatives* - Gold, Pearl • Sepia *Archival* Ink pad • *Gloss Paper*

SUPPLIES: Rubber stamps (*Invoke Arts* Artquotes; *US Artquest* Flower - Dark to Light Background) • *Sizzix* Die cuts (Flower Power, Flower, Daisy) • Lace 3 in 1 Corner punch • Paper Cord • Buttons

INSTRUCTIONS: **Monoprint:** See page 7 for "Monoprint" instructions. Stamp the flower stamp on Gloss Paper for the card background. Die-cut the leaves, flowers and flower paper. Assemble. Adhere buttons to the centers of flowers with Glossy Accents.

Hope
by Nancy Curry
pictured on page 7

SIZE: 6" x 6"

MATERIALS: *Ranger Adirondack* Alcohol Inks used on background - Butterscotch, Stream and Meadow • Alcohol Inks used for Stamp: Wild Plum and Butterscotch • Jet Black *Archival* Ink Pad • White *Gloss Paper*

SUPPLIES: Rubber stamps (*Hero Arts* Long Stemmed Wildflower; *Raindrops Art Stamps* Hope) • Gold Gel Pen - used to outline different areas of intensity and White space borders

INSTRUCTIONS: **Monoprint:** See page 7 for "Monoprint" instructions. Stamp "Hope" and the stems with Black.

Make a Splash
by Nancy Curry

SIZE: 4¼" x 9"

MATERIALS: *Ranger Adirondack* Alcohol Ink - Wild Plum, Terra Cotta, Red Pepper •Copper *Metallic Mixatives* • White *Gloss Paper*

SUPPLIES: Rubber stamp (*Rosie's Roadshow* Make a Splash) • Copper Gel Pen • Black cardstock

INSTRUCTIONS: **Monoprint:** See page 7 for "Monoprint" instructions. Use Red Pepper for the first layer, use Wild Plum and Copper for the second layer of ink. Use a Copper Gel Pen to outline different areas of intensity and boundaries of white space.

Alcohol Ink Monoprinting

by Nancy Curry
technique by Tim Holtz

This technique produces an unusual swirl of colors and metallic. Monoprint: A print that has the same underlying common image, but different design color or texture.

This technique is so versatile, Ranger collected samples from the many graduates of Ranger University Ink and Embossing Powder Certification Course, where this was one of the techniques taught.

Adirondack Alcohol Ink

GENERAL MATERIALS:
Ranger Adirondack: Alcohol Inks; Alcohol Blending Solution; *Metallic Mixatives* • *Inkssentials Non-Stick Craft Sheet* • Jet Black *Archival* ink pad •White *Gloss Paper*

GENERAL INSTRUCTIONS:

Monoprint:
1. Working on the Craft Sheet, apply a squiggle of Metallic Mixatives to the sheet. Note: A little goes a long way. • 2. Add 2-5 colors of Alcohol Inks in lines, dots, etc. directly over the Metallic Mixatives Ink. • 3. Apply a squiggle of Blending Solution. This provides the "slip" for the cardstock and also further mixes together the colors. • 4. Place a piece of gloss cardstock GLOSS SIDE DOWN onto the inks on the Craft Sheet and press, twist in ONE direction, and remove. Wow! Look how the colors and metallic mix and swirl. It dries almost instantly. • 5. For a second-generation print, place more Blending Solution over the leftover inks and make another print in the same direction or try a different twist for a different look. Stamp your images over your background with Jet Black Archival ink pad and let dry.

Tips and Techniques

1. This technique is great for use with your die cutting systems for title letters as well as punches.
2. Use *Cleansit* Stamp Cleaner to clean your Craft Sheet of remaining Alcohol Inks.

1. Squiggle *Metallic Mixatives* or dab an Accent Pen onto a Craft Sheet.

2. Add some *Alcohol Ink* over the *Mixative*.

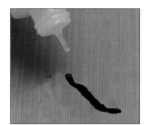

3. Add drops of *Blending Solution*.

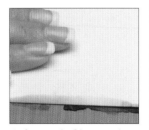

4. Smoosh Gloss side of card into mixture.

5. Repeat smooshing as desired.

Flower Card
by Marie Zaccagnini

SIZE: 4¼" x 4¼"

MATERIALS: *Ranger Adirondack* Alcohol Ink - Denim, Bottle, Lettuce • Craft Sheet • Blending Solution • White *Gloss Paper* - • Copper *Metallic Mixatives* • Jet Black *Archival* Ink

SUPPLIES: Rubber stamps (*Stacy Stamps* SeaGulls; *My Sentiments Exactly* Thinking of You Flowers) Cardstock (Copper, Black) • Ribbon • Rhinestones

INSTRUCTIONS:
1. Place horizontal stripes of Denim Alcohol Ink on the Craft Sheet. • 2. Drop some Blending Solution on the tops of your stripes (if swooshing color from right to left, put Blending Solution on the right edge of your Denim stripes.) • 3. Ink top portion of Gloss Paper. • 4. Place Copper Metallic Mixatives on a different area of the Craft Sheet. • 5. Sprinkle on Bottle and Lettuce Alcohol Inks, followed by Blending Solution. 6. Smoosh the bottom portion of the Gloss Paper, which will create your "land". 7. Stamp seagulls and flowers with Jet Black Archival Ink. • 8. Add rhinestones to the flower centers.

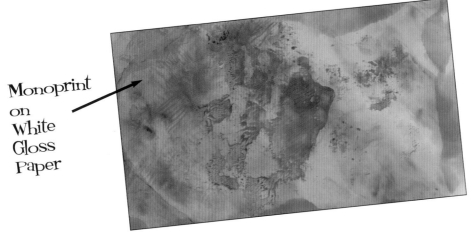

Monoprint
on
White
Gloss
Paper

1. Squeeze some *Alcohol Ink* onto a Craft Sheet.

2. Squeeze drops of *Blending Solution* on *Alcohol Ink.*

3. Drop *Metallic Mixatives* onto the Craft Sheet.

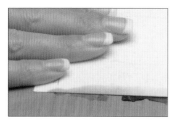

4. Smoosh gloss side of card into mixture.

5. Repeat smooshing as desired. This creates the monoprint.

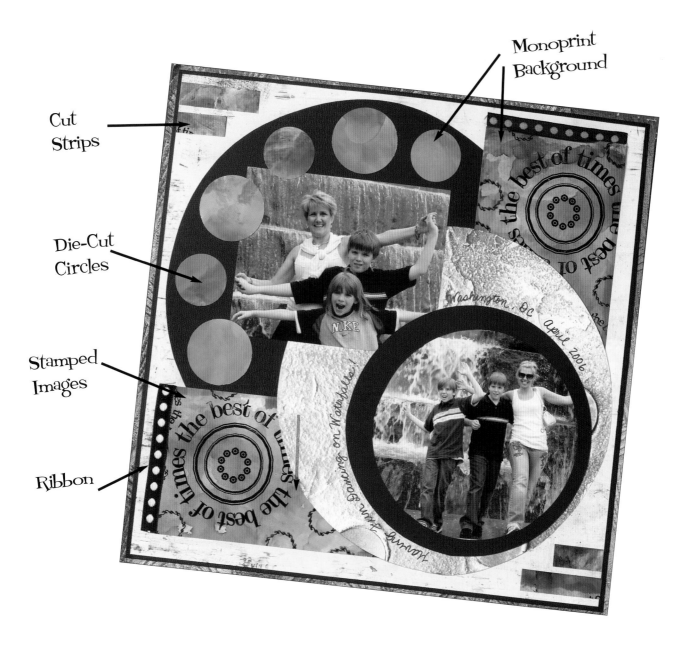

Cut
Strips

Monoprint
Background

Die-Cut
Circles

Stamped
Images

Ribbon

Washington, DC april 2006

the best of times

the best of times

Having fun Bouncing

Bouncing on Waterballs!

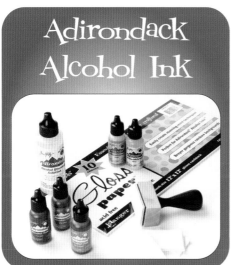

Adirondack Alcohol Ink

The Best of Times
Scrapbook Page
by Patti Behan

SIZE: 12" x 12"

MATERIALS: *Ranger Adirondack:* Alcohol Inks - Denim, Lettuce, Stream; Black *Pigment Pen* • Jet Black *Archival* Ink • White *Gloss Paper*

SUPPLIES: Rubber stamp (*Hampton Arts Danelle Johnson* Memories Interactive Circles) • Pattern papers (*Paperwhite* Novo Egypt, Moon Walk, Shimmer) • Black cardstock • 7" of ½" wide polka dot ribbon

INSTRUCTIONS:

Monoprint: See page 7 for "Monoprint" instructions.

1. Monoprint Gloss Paper with Denim, Lettuce and Stream.
2. When dry, stamp images with Jet Black Archival Ink on monoprint cardstock.
3. Cut two 3½" x 6" pieces from monoprint cardstock. Adhere a 3½" piece of ribbon to one end of each stamped piece.
4. Cut pieces from scraps of monoprint cardstock... 3 circles 1½", 3 circles 1¼" and cut ½" strips.
5. Layer Egypt paper, Black cardstock as the background for the page.
6. Layer the page in this order: large Black circle, stamped pieces, moon walk paper circle, rectangular photo, small Black circle, circle photo and monoprint circles. Add circles cut from monoprint cardstock. Add strips in the corners.
7. Add creative journaling around the circle photo with Pigment Pen.

Tim Holtz Distress Ink

Spot Distress Embossed Tag

by Tim Holtz, technique by Tim Holtz and Fred B. Mullet
Distress Powders are unique. When embossed with embossing ink, such as Distress Embossing Ink, rub off the release crystals for a worn, vintage effect. The matte, textured finish is perfect for weathered effects on scrapbook pages, tags, altered books and frames or boxes.

SIZE: 3⅛" x 6¼"

MATERIALS: *Ranger Tim Holtz Distress Powders* - Vintage Photo, Weathered Wood, Fired Brick, Black Soot • *Tim Holtz Distress Embossing* Ink Stamp Pad • *Tim Holtz Distress Ink Pads* - Aged Mahogany, Broken China, Brushed Corduroy, Tattered Rose, Vintage Photo, Weathered Wood, Antique Linen • Jet Black *Archival* Ink • *Inkssentials Non-Stick Craft Sheet* • *Cut n' Dry Foam* • *Heatit* Craft Tool

SUPPLIES: Manila tag • Ribbon • *Stampers Anonymous* Rubber stamps (Mona Collage, Mistakes)

INSTRUCTIONS:

Stamping: 1. Stamp "Mistakes" image with Jet Black Archival Ink.

Spot Embossing: 2. Apply Embossing Ink to Mona Collage image and stamp onto manila tag. • 3. Shake jars of Distress Powders. Begin with one color and grab a pinch of chosen powder. • 4. Gently "twist" your fingers to allow powder to lightly fall over the area you want to "color". • 5. Repeat with additional colors until image is covered. • 6. Hold tag level off of the table and tap repeatedly with two fingers to allow excess powder to fall off. Do NOT hold tag on end or colors will mix. • 7. Save excess powders in an empty jar as a "party mix". • 8. Heat emboss image with Heatit Tool on the Craft Sheet. Allow to cool.

Distressing Embossed Image: 9. When image is COMPLETELY cooled, gently rub the image with your hand to remove the release crystals. • 10. For an even more distressed look, scrape away more.

Distress with Ink: 11. Apply chosen colors of Distress Inks to foam. • 12. Rub inked foam in a circular motion beginning on the Craft Sheet and pull ink onto the paper to fill inside the image. • 13. Use foam to ink the edges of paper with Antique Linen, Vintage Photo, Brushed Corduroy or other Brown Distress Ink. Work from light to dark colors to make the image "pop".

Tips and Techniques

1. Take your time embossing. *Distress Powders* are a little trickier to see when they have cured. The color of the powder will change in tonal value.

2. Cured *Distress Powder* feels like sandpaper; it's not embossed yet if it feels like sand on the beach.

3. Do not save embossed *Distress Powders* that are rubbed off into your "party mix".

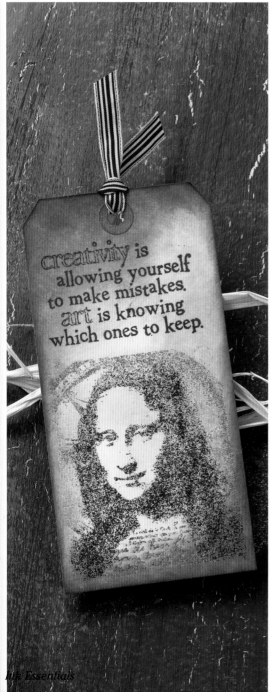

1. Gently twist your fingers to apply powder to desired areas.

2. Holding tag level, tap & carefully turn to allow excess powder to fall off.

Tips and Techniques

This is a great technique for scrapbook pages, borders and especially altered books.

3. Heat emboss the ink to activate the embossing.

4. Gently rub the image to remove excess powder.

5. Apply ink to *Cut n' Dry Foam* & rub on tag in a circular motion.

1. Stamp hotel labels image & smudge.

2. Stamp harlequin image & smudge. Fill in spaces with *Cut 'n Dry Foam.*

Distress Smudge Stamped Tag

by Tim Holtz

When would you ever think that you wanted a stamped image to smudge? Because of the formulation of Distress Ink, it stays wet longer, so the smudging creates a wonderful layered and vintage effect.

SIZE: 3⅛" x 6¼"

MATERIALS: *Ranger Tim Holtz Distress* Ink pads - Aged Mahogany, Antique Linen, Black Soot, Broken China, Brushed Corduroy, Worn Lipstick • *Inkssentials Non-Stick Craft Sheet* • *Cut n' Dry Foam* • Water Mister

SUPPLIES: Manila tag • *Stampers Anonymous* rubber stamps (Hotel Labels, Harlequin, Eiffel Sketch) • Ribbon

INSTRUCTIONS:

1. Cut the foam into squares, one for each color or color group. • 2. Ink Hotel Labels with Aged Mahogany, stamp on tag and immediately smudge ink with square of Cut N' Dry Foam. • 3. Stamp Harlequin with Broken China and smudge. Do the same with the Eiffel Sketch with Black Soot Ink. • 4. Using Cut N' Dry Foam, fill in "spaces" with Antique Linen and Worn Lipstick. • 5. Edge tag with Brushed Corduroy using foam again. • 6. Add ribbon to hole in tag.

Wrinkle-Free Distress Tags

by Tim Holtz

You've got all the colors of the vintage rainbow with the 12 new colors of Distress Ink. Using the wrinkle-free effect, the colors can be layered in a wonderful kaleidoscope of tones.

SIZE: 3⅛" x 6¼"

MATERIALS: *Ranger Tim Holtz Distress* Ink pads - Aged Mahogany, Black Soot, Broken China, Brushed Corduroy, Dried Marigold, Shabby Shutters, Spiced Marmalade, Worn Lipstick • *Inkssentials Non-Stick Craft Sheet* • *Heatit* Craft Tool • *Cut n' Dry Foam* • Water Mister

1. Rub 3 colors of ink onto a *Craft Sheet.*

2. Mist ink on a *Craft Sheet* with water.

3. Press tag into ink on the *Craft Sheet.*

4. Dry tag with a *Heatit* tool.

SUPPLIES: Manila tag • *Stampers Anonymous* Rubber stamps (Dream a Little, Journey, Scratches) • Ribbon • Paper towel

INSTRUCTIONS:

1. Directly apply chosen colors of Distress Ink pads on the Craft Sheet. A couple of swipes of ink will do. Do not overlap the ink colors to avoid muddying the colors. • 2. Liberally spray the inked area of the Craft Sheet with the Water Mister. Allow the inks to blend-Distress Ink reacts with water. 3. Press one side of the tag onto the Craft Sheet to create a "print" of ink. If you have any un-inked areas on the tag simply place back onto the leftover ink on the Craft Sheet. • 4. Dry the tag using the Heatit Tool. Blot off any excess puddle ink or water with a paper towel. • 5. Place inked tag back into the remaining ink on the Craft Sheet and heat again to dry, building layers of color. • 6. Stamp Scratches image with Broken China stamp pad. • 7. Stamp remaining stamps inked with Black Soot onto the tag. • 8. Ink a square of foam with Brushed Corduroy and edge the tag. Note how the foam makes a soft application of ink rather than using the ink pad directly to the tag, which can be more harsh. • 9. Add a ribbon to the hole on the top of the tag.

Accordion Travel Journal

by Michelle Bernard

Glossy Accents is a 3-dimensional, water-based, clear gloss medium. Use it to highlight specific areas on scrapbook pages, cards, stickers, and inside bottle caps.

Place Glossy Accents under embellishments as an adhesive, or on top to protect and glossify.

Tips and Techniques

When applying *Glossy Accents*, try not to lift the nozzle up off of your surface. This will help you to avoid creating air bubbles. If you do get air bubbles, simply use a pin to pop them or drag them to the edge.

1. Trim paper.

2. Cut off corners.

3. Adhere chipboard square to center of cardstock.

4. Fold in sides and glue down.

5. Adhere brown cardstock over folded sides.

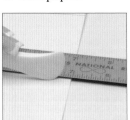

6. Measure and score cardstock for pages.

7. Overlap and glue accordion pages together.

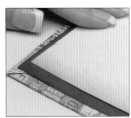

8. Ink the page edges.

9. Spot embellish with *Glossy Accents*.

10. Attach pages to covers.

11. Embellish cover. Glue items with *Glossy Accents*.

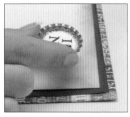

12. Embellish the inside pages.

SIZE: 5" x 5"

MATERIALS: *Ranger Glossy Accents* • Sepia *Archival* Ink pad • *Cut n' Dry Foam* • *Popit! Shapes* ⅛" circles • Silver *Stickles* glitter glue • *Paper Creaser* bone folder • *Perfect Pearls* Pigment Kit Metallics: Perfect Pearl

SUPPLIES: *Design Originals* (*Tim Holtz Distressables* 9" x 9" papers - Two 7" squares of License Plate, 1 Transportation • *Tim Holtz Distressables* doo-dads Light Words • 3 Bottle Caps) • Two 5" squares matboard • Cardstock (White matte, Two 4½" squares Brown, Two 4" x 12" Manila) • 1" circle punch • *Wonder Tape* • Rubber stamps (*River City Rubber Works* Lovells and Gas Station; *Just for Fun* Postcard Background, Memories, New York Tag; *Club Scrap* Distance Scale; *Stampers Anonymous* Paris Map; *Stampendous* Sea Horse; *Delafield Stamp Company* Sand Dollar, Starfish) • *K & Company* Black Label Words & Sayings stickers • *Junkitz* Travel Expressionz rub-ons • *QuicKutz* Die Cuts (Sand Dollar, Olivia Alphabet) • Ephemera • Photos • 28" of Black ribbon • Glue stick

INSTRUCTIONS:

Covers: 1. Center and glue License Plate paper to matboards, wrapping paper over to the back of the board. • 2. Glue Brown squares to the inside of the matboard covers.

Accordion Pages: 3. Fold 1 Manila strip at 4" increments. On the 2nd strip, make a ½" fold, the remaining folds at 4" increments. Cut off the odd length of leftover paper. Glue the ½" flap to the first piece. • 4. Ink a square of foam with Archival Sepia ink and edge the entire set of pages, both sides.

Decorating the Covers: 5. Using the precision, needle-nose applicator on Glossy Accents, highlight a couple of the license plates on both covers. This will create a 3-D look. Let dry. • 6. Cut out the Beetle car from the Transportation paper and glue onto cardboard. Put Popit! Shapes on the back of the car, then apply Glossy Accents to the car. This will make the car look like it was cut from chipboard. Let dry. 7. Computer print words "on the ROAD again" and "travel journal" on White cardstock with Loveletter Typewriter font. Punch out with 1" circle punch and edge paper with foam square inked with Archival Sepia pad. Note: Archival Ink is used because it is waterproof and will not rewet when Glossy Accents is added.

8. Adhere printed words inside bottle caps with Glossy Accents. • 9. Fill each bottle cap with Glossy Accents and set aside to dry.

10. Attach ribbon to front cover with double-sided tape, leaving 8" to the right of the cover so the album can be tied when closed.

11. When all Glossy Accents areas have dried, assemble as shown.

Decorating the inside: 12. Stamp your favorite travel-themed rubber stamps with Archival Sepia ink pad on the front and back of the pages, but not the two "back" pages that will attach to the covers. • 13. Add die cuts, ephemera, photos, doo-dads, rub-ons and stickers. Option: Use Popit! Shapes underneath some of the ephemera for added dimension. • 14. Use the Glossy Accents to emphasize certain areas, to fill bottle caps and embellishments, as well as over rub-ons, doo-dads and stickers.

15. When complete, attach your front and back pages to the covers with Wonder Tape.

'Window' Box

by Michele Charles

This fun 'see-thru window' makes a great top for a box.

SIZE: 5¼" x 5¼"

MATERIALS: *Ranger Glossy Accents*, Inks: *Adirondack* dye, clear embossing, *Archival* Sepia and Jet Black; Gold embossing powder

SUPPLIES: Rubber stamps (*Magenta, Judikins, Above the Mark*) • 2 Transparency sheets 5" x 5" • *Modern Options* Copper paint, Green Patina • 5 Black foam core squares 5¼" x 5¼" • Craft knife • Collage images • Cardstock (Black, White) • Stipple brush • Colored pencils • Chipboard window die cut • Velcro

INSTRUCTIONS:

Patina Cardstock: Stamp and emboss text in Gold embossing powder on 2 pieces of Black cardstock and die-cut window. Cover with Copper paint. Let dry. Apply Green Patina to painted surface. Let dry.

Collage: 1. Cut a 4¼" square from center of four foam core pieces to create frames. • 2. Adhere collage images to Black cardstock. Cut out images leaving a ¼" tab on side that attaches to frame. Adhere image to two frames. 3. Stipple *Adirondack* dye ink on 5" x 5" cardstock. Adhere to center of solid foam core board. • 4. Stamp coat of arms in Jet Black ink. Color, cut and adhere to background. 5. Stamp text on transparency in Sepia ink. Adhere to frame. 6. Adhere transparency frame on top of background piece. Adhere other two frames on top.

Window: 7. Cover transparency with a thin layer of Glossy Accents. Press Glossy Accents side onto rubber stamp. Press firmly so Glossy Accents flows into crevices of stamp. Remove transparency. Let dry. Wash Glossy Accents from rubber stamp immediately. • 8. Adhere transparency to back of window. • 9. Adhere window to last frame.

Hinge: 10. Cut 5¼" x 1" strip of Green Patina cardstock. Adhere to left edge of window frame. Adhere hinge to left side of box.

Box: 11. Cover sides of box and window frame with Patina cardstock. Cut two 5¼" x 5¼" cardstock pieces. Cut 4¼" square from center. Adhere to top of box and back of window.

Latch: 12. Cut small strip of Patina cardstock. Fold over ½" on one end. Adhere to window side. Stamp key hole in black ink and color. Cut out. Adhere to strip. Attach Velcro to back of strip and side of box.

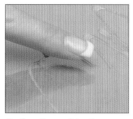

1. Apply a thin layer of *Glossy Accents* to a transparency sheet.

2. Press the rubber stamp onto wet *Glossy Accents* to make a texture.

Juggling Clown Card

by Michelle Bernard

Archival Ink is ideal for stamping on Inkssentials Gloss Paper, and coloring with dye inks such as Adirondack, Distress Ink and (as in this card) Nick Bantock Dye Ink.

Archival Ink is an oil-based ink that doesn't smear when you color over it. You can make any ink pad into a marker with the use of Cut 'n Dry pen nibs.

SIZE: 5" x 7"

MATERIALS: *Ranger Nick Bantock* Collection Stamp Pads - Cerulean Azure, Chrome Yellow, Rose Madder • Jet Black *Archival* Ink pad • Turquoise *Stickles* Glitter Glue • *Popit! Shapes* 1/8" Circles • 7" x 10" *Gloss Paper* pre-scored card • *Cut n' Dry* - Foam & Pen Nibs • *Inkssentials* Non-Stick Craft Sheet

SUPPLIES: Rubber stamps (*Stampers Anonymous* Celestial Clown; *Hero Arts* Old French Writing) • Cutting Mat • Awl • *Artistic Wire* Silver 24 ga. wire • Wire cutters • Brads

INSTRUCTIONS:
1. Stamp clown onto Gloss Paper with Jet Black Archival Ink, set aside.
2. Take another sheet of pre-scored Gloss Paper, lay it onto your Craft Sheet. Cut a square of foam, tap into the Rose Madder Nick Bantock Ink several times.
3. Rub foam onto the right side of card in a circular motion. Continue to re-ink the foam and apply to the Gloss Paper until the entire right side is covered. Set this aside. • 4. Take a pen nib and roll the tip into Cerulean Azure Ink. Color in the appropriate parts on clown. Using a new nib, do the same for the stars and moons using Chrome Yellow, and the cheeks using Rose Madder. • 5. Cut out pieces of the clown. On a craft mat, lay out body, arms and legs as desired.

6. Using an awl, make a hole for brads. Assemble pieces together with brads. Also make a hole in each hand for inserting the juggling balls later. • 7. Stamp Old French Writing stamp onto the front of card using Jet Black Archival Ink. Let dry. • 8. Remove one side of backing of Popit! Shapes. Adhere two on the back of clown's body and one on the back of each leg. Don't use any on the arms, as you want them to be movable. • 9. Position clown over front of card, remove Popit! Shapes backing and adhere. • 10. Cut a 7" piece of wire, bend into a U shape. • 11. Take two circle Popit! Shapes and peel off the protective backing on one side. Adhere circles sticky side together, sandwiching U-shaped wire in between. Repeat two times to create three juggling balls. • 12. Remove protective backings of Popit! Shapes on one side, color with Turquoise Stickles. Let dry, color the sides and back of Popit! Shapes with Stickles. When dry, attach wire to clown.

1. Stamp the image.

2. Tap foam into Rose Madder ink.

3. Rub inked foam on right-hand side of card.

4. Roll tip of a nib into Cerulean Azure.

5. Color the stamped image with nib.

6. Cut out the colored image.

7. Attach clown parts together with brads.

8. Bend wire, sandwich it between 2 *Popits*.

9. Embellish with *Stickles*.

10. Attach wire to the clown's hands.

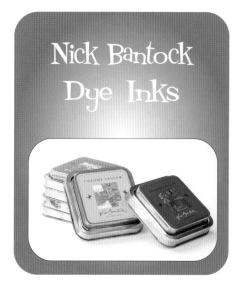

Nick Bantock Dye Inks

Watercolor With Dye Inks
by Robin Beam

Water-based dye ink stamp pads such as Adirondack, Nick Bantock and Distress, to name a few are perfect for watercolor techniques.

SIZE:
Friends Card $6\frac{3}{4}$" x 7"
Queen Card $6\frac{1}{4}$" x $6\frac{1}{4}$"
Ferris Wheel Card $6\frac{3}{4}$" x $6\frac{7}{8}$"

GENERAL MATERIALS: *Ranger Nick Bantock* Collection Stamp Pads • *Inkssentials Non-Stick Craft Sheet* • *Heatit* Craft Tool • Jet Black *Archival* Ink pad • *Popit! Shapes* $\frac{1}{8}$" Square • Water Mister

GENERAL SUPPLIES: *Niji* Waterbrush • 140# Watercolor paper • Glue stick

INDIVIDUAL MATERIALS:

Friends Card: Rubber stamps (*Paperbag Studios* Always Young, Prosperity) • *Design Originals - Tim Holtz* 9" x 9" Mother Goose cardstock

Queen Card: Rubber stamps (*Stampers Anonymous* Queen of Staves, I was Queen) • *K & Co.* Life's Journey 6" x 6" Ruler Pad • Black cardstock

Ferris Wheel Card: Rubber stamps (*Club Scrap* County Fair Ferris Wheel; *Stampendous* Enjoy) • *Arctic Frog* Sunday Brunch Lily Pads paper

GENERAL INSTRUCTIONS:

1. Stamp image with Jet Black ink pad on watercolor paper. Let dry or use Heatit Tool to speed drying. TIP: Archival Ink is a dye ink, but with an oil-based formulation that when dry, is waterproof, thus is perfect for techniques where you want to use water. • 2. Take a Nick Bantock stamp pad, rub a corner of it on the Craft Sheet. You will use this as your ink "palette". • 3. Pick up ink with a waterbrush. If you want to have a lighter tone, squeeze a bit of water from waterbrush next to the ink and mix it. The more water mixed with ink, the lighter tone it will be. The less water added, the more intense it will look. • 4. Paint in image. If the color is too dark on the paper, clean the tip of waterbrush and "pick up" some color with clean water from the brush. • 5. Dry the painted area quickly with the Heatit Tool. This way you will "freeze" the watercolor effect. • 6. When finished painting in the image there will be various "puddles" of color on the Craft Sheet. Pick up colors with the waterbrush and tap color onto image, splattering small dots of color. Dry with Heatit Tool. • 7. For background papers follow instructions for the "Wrinkle Free" Distress Technique **on page 11** using Nick Bantock Ink colors. • 8. Layer the cards. For added dimension use Popit! Shapes beneath some of the layers.

Tips and Techniques

1. You don't have to use expensive watercolor paper. Just about any cold press paper will be fine. In fact, don't use paper that is too textured, as certain images will not stamp clearly.

2. *Archival Ink* is the perfect ink to use with water-based dye markers, as water in the markers will not rewet the ink from the rubber stamped image.

3. If there is too much water on your watercolor surface, use a clean piece of paper towel and soak up the excess water.

1. Rub a corner of the ink pad onto a *Craft Sheet.*

2. Pick up rubbed ink with a waterbrush.

3. Paint image with a waterbrush.

4. Heat set image to 'freeze' the watercolor effect.

5. Splatter image by tapping waterbrush on your finger.

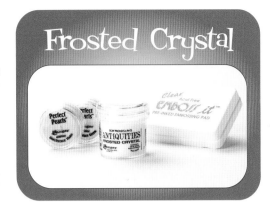

Frosted Crystal

Angel Card: 'Two Looks'

by Debbie Tlach
One of the most "magical" and multi-purpose Embossing Powders is Ranger's Embossing Antiquities Frosted Crystal.

When embossed it has a matte, textured finish. When embossed over a stamped image it looks and feels like etched glass. When Perfect Pearls Pigment powders are brushed over the top, the texture allows the Perfect Pearls to stick, resulting in a raku-type of finish.

SIZE: 3⅛" x 4½"
MATERIALS: *Ranger* Frosted Crystal *Embossing Antiquities* • Clear Embossing Powder • *Adirondack Pigment Pens* • Jet Black *Archival* Ink pad •White *Gloss Paper* • *Emboss it* Clear Embossing Pad • *Inkssentials Non-Stick Craft Sheet* • Small *Perfect Brush* • *Heatit* Craft Tool
SUPPLIES: Black cardstock • Rubber stamp (*Stampers Anonymous* Angel Collage) • Glue stick • Water
INSTRUCTIONS:
1. Ink stamp with Jet Black Archival Ink. Stamp onto Gloss Paper. Use Heatit Tool to dry ink thoroughly. • 2. Scribble pens onto Craft Sheet. • 3. Dip small brush in water and into scribbled ink and color in the stamped image. Use Heatit Tool to dry thoroughly. Cut out painted image. • 4. Using the Emboss it Pad directly to paper, apply ink to the entire image. • 5. Depending on what type of finish you desire, pour clear (for a shiny finish) or Frosted Crystal (for a matte, "etched glass" finish) over the inked image. • 6. Emboss with Heatit Tool. Let cool. • 7. Cut and fold Black cardstock. Adhere embossed image to card.

Crystal 'Hearts' Card

by Robin Beam
SIZE: 5¼" x 8¾"
MATERIALS: *Ranger* Frosted Crystal *Embossing Antiquities* • *Inkssentials Non-Stick Craft Sheet* • *Heatit* Craft Tool • *Popit! Shapes* ⅛" Squares • Clear *Perfect Medium* Pad • *Perfect Pearls* Pigment powders - Blush, Kiwi, Perfect Pearl, Sunflower Sparkle, Turquoise • *Perfect Brushes* • 5¼" x 8¾" card - White *Gloss Paper*
SUPPLIES: Rubber stamps (*Hero Arts* Paisley Prints, Paisley Heart, Moments) • 2 sheets 8½" x 11" Black matte cardstock • Soft cloth or paper towel • Glue stick • Scissors
INSTRUCTIONS:
1. On 1 sheet of Black cardstock, stamp 5 Paisley Hearts with Clear Perfect Medium.
2. Sprinkle on Frosted Crystal powder. Shake off excess and return to jar. • 3. Emboss images with Heatit Tool. • 4. Brush embossed Paisley Hearts with chosen colors of Perfect Pearls Pigment powders. Brush off excess Perfect Pearls with larger Perfect Brush and a soft cloth or paper towel. • 5. Cut out hearts and set aside. • 6. Cut Black cardstock 5⅛" x 8½".
7. Randomly stamp paisley images with Perfect Medium Pad. On bottom right hand side of cardstock stamp "moments". • 8. With detail brush, pick up chosen color of Perfect Pearls Pigment powders and dust on stamped images.
9. Brush off excess with larger whisk brush.
10. Attach 3 of the hearts with Glue stick and 2 with Popit! Shapes for added dimension.
11. Layer onto 5¼" x 8¾" glossy card.

1. Brush *Perfect Pearls* onto embossed area.

2. Use a large whisk brush to brush off excess powder.

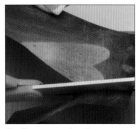

3. Cut out the hearts.

Clear Embossing   Frosted Crystal

Crystal 'Dream' Card

by Debbie Tlach

SIZE: 4⅛" x 5⅛"

MATERIALS: *Ranger* Frosted Crystal *Embossing Antiquities* • Embossing Powder - Clear, Queen's Gold, Black *Super Fine Detail* • *Emboss it* Clear Embossing Pad • *Heatit* Craft Tool • Diamond *Stickles* Glitter Glue • *Inkssentials* Non-Stick Craft Sheet • *Popit! Shapes*

SUPPLIES: Rubber stamps (*Fred B. Mullett* Kemuri Visual Vapor, *Art Impressions* Dream) • Cardstock (Burgundy: 4" x 5", 1" x 3¾"; Black: 3½" x 4½", 4⅛" x 5⅛") • Glue stick

INSTRUCTIONS:
1. Ink Kemuri stamp with the Emboss it Pad. Stamp onto 3½" x 4½" Black cardstock.
2. Working over the Craft Sheet, shake Clear Embossing Powder onto selected areas of image. • 3. Carefully pick up card and turn face down very quickly to remove excess powder from the image. This preserves areas with ink and no powder. Return excess powder to jar. • 4. Shake Frosted Crystal Embossing Powder onto the image. Carefully tap off excess and return to jar. • 5. Heat emboss with Heatit Tool. • 6. Run the edges of the card across the Emboss it Pad.
7. Pour about ¼ of a jar of Queen's Gold Embossing Powder onto the Craft Sheet.
8. Dip the inked edges into the Embossing Powder. Remove excess powder by tapping the back of the card and carefully using a fine brush to remove any excess powder.
9. Ink "Dream" stamp with the Emboss it Pad. Stamp onto 1" x 3¾" Burgundy card-stock. • 10. Emboss image with Black Super Fine Detail Embossing Powder. • 11. Edge the card with Queen's Gold Embossing Powder as shown in step 7. Mount Black embossed cardstock to 4" x 5" Burgundy mat. Adhere to 4⅛" x 5⅛" Black cardstock.
12. Place Popit! Shapes beneath the Dream image.

Tips and Techniques

Perfect Pearls Pigment powders have a built-in binder. *Perfect Medium* is specially formulated to work with *Perfect Pearls* and no fixative is needed. To further ensure that *Perfect Pearls* dusted on *Perfect Medium* will not come off, spritz with a light mist of water.

1. Stamp image with *Emboss it* ink.

2. Shake clear embossing powder onto select areas.

3. Tap off the excess powder.

4. Shake on Frosted Crystal to remaining inked areas.

5. Tap off excess powder.

6. Emboss card with *Heatit* tool.

7. Ink edge as with *Emboss it* Ink pad.

8. Shake out Queen's Gold embossing powder onto Craft Sheet.

9. Run edges of card through Queen's Gold Embossing Powder.

10. Accent random areas with Diamond *Stickles*.

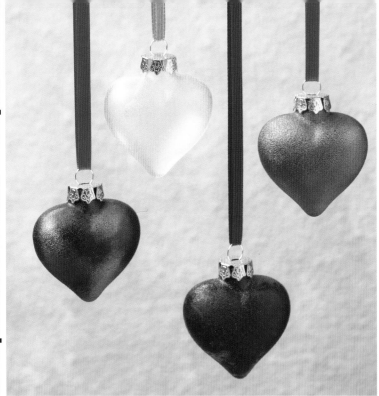

Frosted Crystal Frame

by Chris Herrmann

SIZE: 2⅞" x 3⅞"

MATERIALS: *Ranger Emboss it* Clear Embossing Pad • *Embossing Antiquities* Frosted Crystal • *Heatit* Craft Tool • *Cut n' Dry Foam* • *Perfect Pearls* Pigment Kits - Naturals: Kiwi; Interference: Violet, Blue, Green; Aged Patina: Heirloom Gold • *Perfect Brushes*

SUPPLIES: Rubber stamp (*Just For Fun* Lepidoptera) • 2⅞" x 3⅞" Beveled Mini Frame • Black cardstock

INSTRUCTIONS:

1. Apply Clear Embossing Ink to frame. • 2. Sprinkle on Frosted Crystal Embossing Powder. Shake off excess and return to jar. • 3. Heat emboss with Heatit Tool. • 4. Follow same process on Black cardstock with rubber stamp. • 5. Brush on colors of Perfect Pearls pigment powders with detail brush. Remove excess powder with a brush. • 6. Trim cardstock to fit frame.

Frosted Crystal Glass Ornaments

by Chris Herrmann

SIZE: 2½" x 2½"

MATERIALS: *Ranger Emboss it* Clear Embossing Pad • *Cut n' Dry Foam* • Frosted Crystal *Embossing Antiquities* • *Heatit* Craft Tool • Pitch Black *Adirondack* Alcohol Ink • *Perfect Pearls* Pigment Kits - Jewels: Forever Red; Interference: Interference Red; Pastels: Sunflower Sparkle • *Perfect Brushes*

SUPPLIES: Heart-shaped glass ornaments

INSTRUCTIONS:

1. Remove cap and hook from ornament. • 2. Apply Clear Embossing ink to front of glass using a square of foam. 3. Sprinkle on Frosted Crystal Powder. Shake off excess and return to jar. • 4. Emboss with Heatit tool. Let cool. • 5. Repeat process on opposite side.

Black Ornament:

6. Place drops of Pitch Black Alcohol Ink inside and swirl around to cover interior surface. Pour out excess.

Pearly Ornaments:

7. Apply Perfect Pearls with a small brush. Because Frosted Crystal Powder has a matte and textured finish, Perfect Pearls sticks to the embossed surface. Brush off excess powder with larger brush. • 8. Replace cap and hook.

Trinket Box

by Chris Herrmann

SIZE: 2½" x 3½" x 1½" tall

MATERIALS:

Ranger Black *Decor it* ink • *Emboss it* Clear Embossing Pad • Frosted Crystal *Embossing Antiquities* • *Heatit* Craft Tool • *Cut n' Dry Foam* • *Perfect Pearls* Pigment Kits - Jewels: Forever Violet; Aged Patina: Blue Patina; Pastels: Sunflower Sparkle • *Perfect Brushes*

SUPPLIES: Rubber stamps (*Another Stamp Company* Shell #1 Scallop, Sun & Starfish Cube) • Oval paper mache box

INSTRUCTIONS:

1. Shake up Black Decor it ink, squeeze some out onto a square of foam. • 2. Pat inked foam onto box, covering top and bottom. Let dry. 3. Ink Scallop stamp with Clear Embossing ink, stamp onto top of box. • 4. Shake on Frosted Crystal Embossing Powder and shake off excess, returning to jar. • 5. Heat emboss with Heatit Tool. • 6. Repeat process with small starfish stamp around the bottom of box. 7. Using smaller, detail Perfect Brush, brush on Perfect Pearls Pigment powders. • 8. Remove excess pigment powders with larger, whisk Perfect brush. • 9. Option: For a finished look, line inside of box with decorative paper.

1. Squeeze *Decorit* onto *Cut n' Dry Foam*.

2. Pat inked foam onto box.

3. Shake on Frosted Crystal powder.

4. Emboss with *HeatIt* tool.

5. Brush on *Perfect Pearls*.

6. Brush off excess with a large brush.

Posh Impressions Rainbow Sponge

Two-Tone Rainbow Sponge Background
by Robin Beam

This is a wonderful way to incorporate metallic shimmer with the full colors of dye inks in Rainbow Sponge Kits. This is ideal to use for scrapbook pages and cards where bold images are needed.

SIZE: Giggle card: 5" x 7"; Journey card: 6" x 7", Tree card: 5½" x 8½"; Tag on page 2: 2⅝" x 4½"

MATERIALS: *Ranger Posh Impressions* - Posh Rainbow Sponge & Ink Kits: Earthtones or Floral Brights; Posh *Metallic Inkabilities*: Precious Metals or Luminous Metallics; Posh 4-Count Sponge Kit • Black Embossing Powder • *Two-Tone Big & Bossy* Embossing Pad • White matte cardstock • *Inkssentials Non-Stick Craft Sheet* • *Heatit* Craft Tool

SUPPLIES: Rubber stamps (Tree Card: *Just For Fun* Tree Block, Ironwork Tag; Giggle Card: *Paperbag Studios* Laugh, *Stampers Anonymous* Giggle; Journey Tree Card: *Just For Fun* Tree Line, *Stampers Anonymous* Journey; *Another Stamp Company* Travel Words) • Matte Copper Buttonz • *Junkitz Tim Holtz* Epoxy Stickerz

INSTRUCTIONS:
1. Using the small rectangle sponge from the 4-Count Sponge Set, use various colors of Metallic Inkabilities on the small, square end. • 2. On the matte White cardstock, "tile" the Metallic Inkabilities inked sponge; you can use a random pattern, or a harlequin or checkerboard design. 3. Blot on scrap paper or let air dry. • 4. Ink up sponge from the Earthtone or Floral Brights Kit. • 5. Swipe the inked Rainbow Sponge across the paper. Note how the Metallic Inkabilities "resists" through the dye inks. Blot any excess ink off the Metallic Inkabilities design if you want the metallic to "pop" more. • 6. Dry paper with Heatit Tool. This is an important step because the matte paper absorbs a lot of ink, so you need to be sure it is dry before the next step. • 7. Ink chosen stamp with the Black pigment ink side of the Two-Tone Big & Bossy Embossing Pad. • 8. Stamp inked image on paper and emboss with Black Embossing Powder. Emboss with Heatit Tool. • 9. Trim image and layer onto cardstock.

Tips and Techniques

1. *Rainbow Sponge Kits* work ideally on *Gloss Paper* as the clay coating on the paper doesn't absorb as much ink.

2. *Metallic Inkabilities* work on non-porous surfaces such as *UTEE*, wood, Shrink Plastic as well as dark matte and/or *Gloss Paper*.

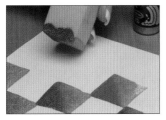

1. Use a sponge to stamp *Metallic Inkabilities* in a checkerboard pattern.

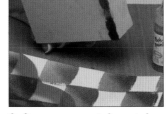

2. Sponge on rainbow ink in a wavy pattern.

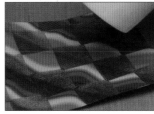

3. Heat set the ink colors.

4. Stamp images and emboss with *Heatit* tool.

1. Roll ink over resist stamped image.

Big and Juicy Birthday Card
by Robin Beam

Big & Juicy Rainbow Pads are 3" x 6" large, hand-made stamp pads full of color. Color is placed side by side in the felt pad so that when stamped or brayered, color softly transitions from one to the other.

They are perfect for creating rainbows of color as well as in stamping and making resist backgrounds. When smaller images are stamped with a Rainbow Pad, it's like having 6 or more colors in one.

SIZE: 4½" x 5¾"

MATERIALS: *Ranger* Vibrant Primary *Big & Juicy* Rainbow Pad • *Inky Roller* large brayer • 8½" x 11" White *Gloss Paper* • *Clear Resist* Pad • Jet Black *Archival* Ink pad • *Heatit* Craft Tool

SUPPLIES: Rubber stamps (*Another Stamp Company* Candles; *Hero Arts* Wavy Wishes, Quatros Pinwheels) • 4½" x 5¾" Black card • Paper towel • Scrap paper

INSTRUCTIONS:
1. Cut Gloss Paper 4¼" x 5½" and 2¾" x 5½". • 2. Place large rectangle on scrap paper. • 3. Ink pinwheel images with Clear Resist ink, stamp on Gloss Paper. Dry with a Heatit Tool. • 4. Open up Rainbow Pad, turn Inky Roller brayer so that the "feet" are up (brakes off). • 5. Thoroughly ink up roller. Be sure to lift up roller and that the entire roller gets inked. Don't just move it back and forth, as you will not get full ink coverage on the roller. • 6. With the Gloss Paper longest side horizontal to you, place the inked brayer down on the paper and begin to roll the color on. • 7. Reink the brayer and continue to apply ink to the Gloss Paper until you get even coverage on the paper. • 8. Take a clean paper or cloth towel and working from lighter to darker colors, wipe off excess ink. • 9. Ink up Candles stamp using the same Vibrant Primary Rainbow stamp pad. Firmly press down on the other piece of Gloss Paper. • 10. Use a Heatit Tool to dry ink. Adhere to resist rainbow background. • 11. With Jet Black pad, repeatedly stamp "Happy Birthday" image above and below the candles image. • 12. Layer on Black card with a glue stick.

Tips and Techniques

1. For a brighter, more batik-like resisted image, use *Perfect Medium* Pad.

2. Never store *Big & Juicy* Rainbow Pads on their sides. Gravity will pull the dye inks down and muddy the colors.

3. Save the bottom label on *Big & Juicy* Rainbow Pads. The colors are listed in order on this label, which is helpful when you want to reink.

4. If you live in a very humid area, keep Rainbow Pads in the refrigerator to prevent the ink from moving.

5. To avoid getting "lines" on the paper, brayer off of the cardstock. Every time you "stop" on the paper, it will create a line. If you get a line, just work more ink into the paper and it will disappear.

6. The *Craft Sheet* is not recommended as a brayering surface because you end up with a lot of ink sliding around. A scrap paper base gives you better control of the brayer.

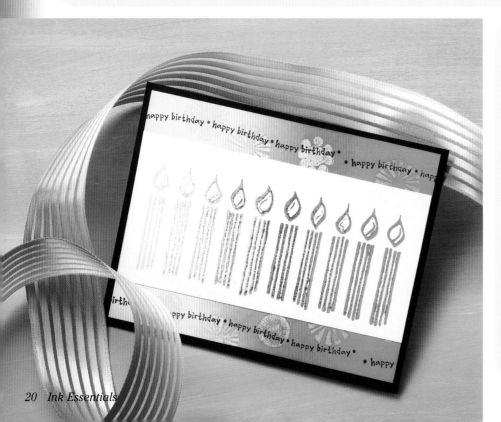

More Tips and Techniques

1. When using rainbow pads, be sure to brayer in a vertical direction, staying within the path of the color on the ink pad, so that the ink colors stay true.

2. Ranger's *Inky Brayers* provide a wonderful surface for creating different patterns for inking and rolling. Try *Popit! Shapes*, interesting fibers, masking tape in random designs – use your imagination.

3. A light application of color when using objects on the brayer creates one look. Apply more ink and create another look that can be incorporated into a coordinated scrapbook page or card.

4. Ranger's *Inky Rollers* are carvable and replacement rollers are available to dedicate a design to each one.

5. Each *Scrapbooker's Palette* ink pad contains 4 cells of *Archival* waterproof ink. There are 3 different *Scrapbooker's Palette* ink pads for a collection of 12 *Archival Ink* colors.

Rainbow 'Dream' Card

by Robin Beam and Bonnie Egenton

SIZE: 5" x 5¾"

MATERIALS: *Ranger* Vibrant Primary *Big & Juicy* Rainbow Pad • *Clear Resist* Pad • Black Embossing Powder • *Gloss Paper* • *Heatit* Craft Tool • *Big & Bossy* Two-Tone Embossing Pad • *Inky Roller* medium brayer • *Popit! Shapes* ⅛" Squares • Cardstock - White matte, Black

SUPPLIES: Rubber stamps (*Hampton Art Stamps* Swirls; *Stampers Anonymous* Fairies Cube, Carved Swirl, Dream) • Glue stick

INSTRUCTIONS:

1. Ink swirls rubber stamp with Clear Resist Pad and stamp on Gloss Paper in a checkerboard pattern. Either air dry, blot dry on scrap paper or use Heatit Tool to dry. • 2. Open up Big & Juicy Rainbow Pad and turn Inky Roller brayer so that the feet are up (brakes off). • 3. Thoroughly ink up roller using the left side of the rainbow stamp pad. Be sure to lift up roller so that the entire roller gets inked. Don't just move it back and forth, as you will not get full ink coverage on the roller. • 4. Place the inked brayer down on the paper and begin to roll the color on. After fully inking that strip, reink the brayer and ink the next section. Repeat until the entire area is inked with stripes. • 5. Turn the paper and repeat steps 3-4, but use the middle area of the rainbow ink pad. This will create a plaid. • 6. Use a clean paper or towel to rub off any excess ink. See how the resisted image just pops. • 7. Ink carved swirl stamp with the Black pigment ink side of the Big & Bossy pad and stamp onto Gloss Paper. 8. Sprinkle on Black Embossing Powder. Shake off excess and return to jar.

1. Layer ink for a plaid effect.

9. Heat emboss with Heatit Tool. Trim so there is a slight border around the image. • 10. On White matte cardstock stamp three of the fairy images with the rainbow pad. Stamp images so you are using the single colors from the rainbow pad. Just think - you have 6 colors in one pad. Cut out. • 11. Layer plaid brayered cardstock onto Black cardstock with glue stick. 12. Glue carved swirl image to top portion of brayered cardstock. • 13. Use Popit! Shapes to 3-D fairies on carved swirl image. • 14. Stamp "dream" with Black pigment ink and heat emboss with Heatit Tool.

Conversations Between Friends Card

by Robin Beam and Bonnie Egenton

See how versatile and color-rich Ranger's dye inks can be when using an Inky Roller in multiple ways.

SIZE: 5½" x 8½"

MATERIALS: *Ranger* Jet Black *Archival* Ink pad • *Clear Resist* Pad • 2 sheets 8½" x 11" *Gloss Paper* • *Inky Roller* brayer - Small, Large • Mountain Meadow *Big & Juicy* Rainbow Pad • Brights *Scrapbooker's Palette* ink pad • *Tim Holtz Distress Ink* pads - Scattered Straw, Faded Jeans, Spiced Marmalade, Tea Dye, Black Soot • *Cut n' Dry Nibs* • *Heatit* Craft Tool • *Popit! Shapes* ⅛" Circles

SUPPLIES: Rubber stamp (*Paperbag Studios* Silences) • *Junkitz Tim Holtz* Rounderz • *Wonder Tape* • Rubber bands • Scrap paper • Paper or cloth towel

INSTRUCTIONS:

1. Fold sheet of Gloss Paper in half to create a card. • 2. Using Large Inky Roller, wrap small bubble wrap around the brayer and adhere with Red tape. 3. Using Mountain Meadow Big & Juicy Rainbow Pad, roll the bubble-wrapped brayer across the ink pad in one direction and lifting up each time to ensure complete ink coverage. • 4. Brayer across the front of the Gloss Paper card until you get the desired color coverage. To get deeper color, reink the brayer and roll on the card again. Set aside to dry. • 5. Wrap a small Inky Roller with rubber bands. Ink brayer with Clear Resist and roll across a small piece of Gloss Paper. On scrap paper, brayer off any remaining ink. Heat set the ink with the Heatit Tool. • 6. Using Scrapbooker's Palette, brayer with Banana and brayer Gloss Paper again. On scrap paper, brayer off remaining ink. Repeat with Tangerine, Aqua, and Carnation on the Gloss Paper. It looks like streamers. • 7. Using small Inky Roller without rubber bands, brayer Black Soot Distress Ink over the rubber band ink design. With a soft cotton cloth or paper towel, buff off excess ink and see the Archival inked colors also resist through the dye ink. • 8. Cut into strips and adhere to right side of card, spacing the strips randomly. • 9. Add a Tim Holtz Rounderz to the bottom strip of paper before gluing down. Set aside. • 10. On another piece of Gloss Paper stamp "Silences" image with Jet Black Archival Ink. Heat set with Heatit Tool.

1. Roll an inked rubber-banded brayer over cardstock.

2. Roll on Black ink.

11. Using nibs, color in hair with Scattered Straw and Tea Dye Distress Inks using a small circular motion for even coverage. Color in tee shirts and jeans in Spiced Marmalade and Faded Jeans Distress Inks. • 12. Adhere to center of card with Popit! Shapes.

UTEE Brightz

UTEE Makes a Raised Area of Embossing

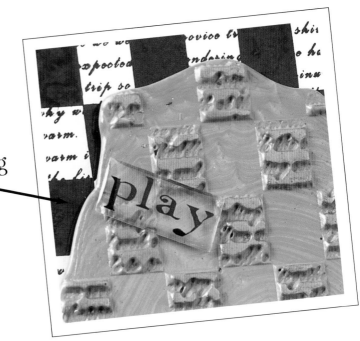

Tips and Techniques

1. One color of *UTEE* does not have to be melted in the *Melting Pot*. You can melt a couple of colors and pour it out.

Let it melt without stirring it. When poured, see the swirl of color that is created.

2. For bright transparent color, use clear and To Dye For Colorants; for bright opaque color, use *UTEE* Brightz.

3. Don't stir the *UTEE* as it will cause bubbles in the *UTEE* and in your Melt Art piece!

UTEE Brightz Card

by Robin Beam & Bonnie Egenton, technique by Suze Weinberg
UTEE is so much fun and with the UTEE Brightz colors, you can "play" with the vibrant and pearlescent colors on cards and scrapbook pages.

SIZE: 5" x 6"
MATERIALS: *Ranger* Green Zinnia *UTEE Brightz* • Jet Black *Archival* Ink pad • *Big & Bossy* Clear Embossing Pad • Gold *Metallic Mixatives* • Inkssentials Non-Stick Craft Sheet • *Melting Pot* • White *Gloss Paper* • *Glossy Accents* • *Cleansit* Stamp Cleaner

SUPPLIES: Rubber stamp (*Stampers Anonymous* Checkerboard Corner) • *Junkitz - Tim Holtz* Expressions Black Epoxy Stickerz • Cardstock (Black, Green) • Mahjong tile

INSTRUCTIONS:
1. Turn the Melting Pot to the UTEE setting. Pour Green Zinnia UTEE Brightz into the pan and place lid on top to allow to melt.
2. Ink stamp with Clear Embossing Ink and place rubber side up on the Craft Sheet.
3. Once UTEE Brightz has completely melted, pour onto the rubber stamp, but avoid it pouring onto the wood portion of the rubber stamp. Allow to cool. • 4. While the UTEE is still a touch warm, but able to be handled, peel off of the rubber. Rub Gold Metallic Mixative over UTEE with your finger. • 5. Clean off embossing ink from the stamp with Cleansit and ink it with Jet Black Archival Ink. Stamp onto Gloss Paper. Trim leaving a border. • 6. Layer onto Black and Green cardstock. • 7. Glue UTEE Brightz image onto layered cardstock with Glossy Accents. 8. Glue Mahjong tile onto bottom right rectangle with Glossy Accents. • 9. Stick on "play" Epoxy Stickerz to the UTEE.

UTEE Brightz
Dipped Memory Glass Pins

by Robin Beam,
technique by Suze Weinberg

The wonderful colors of UTEE Brightz make these pins pop. Use a stamp for both the stamped image and stamping into the UTEE to create a dimensional masterpiece.

SIZE: Floral Pin: 1½" x 3½"; Shy Eye Pin: 1¾" x 1¾"

MATERIALS: *Ranger UTEE* Brightz - Fuchsia, Violet • *Melting Pot* • *Melt Art - Non-Stick Craft Sheet, Kool Toolz* • *Memory Glass* - Two 1" x 3"; Two 2" x 2" • *Big & Bossy* Clear Embossing Pad • *Cleansit* Stamp Cleaner • *Glossy Accents* • Purple Rain *BeaDazzles* • Silver *Adirondack Metallic Mixatives* • *Nick Bantock* Collection Stamp Pads - Cerulean Azure, Chartreuse Leaf, Chrome Yellow, Damson Plum, Deep Turquoise, Rose Madder, Sapmoss Green, Vermillion Lacquer, Van Dyke Brown • Jet Black *Archival* Ink pad

SUPPLIES: Rubber stamps (*Just For Fun* Large Dandelion, Those Eyes; *Stampers Anonymous* Crewel Border) • White matte cardstock - 1" x 3", 2" x 2" • *Niji* Waterbrush • Pin backs

INSTRUCTIONS:

Floral Pin: 1. Stamp Floral Border with Jet Black Archival Ink onto cut matte cardstock. Stamp image to line up with the top ⅔ of the glass. Clean off with Cleansit. Stamp image again into Clear Embossing Ink Stamp Pad and set aside. • 2. Swipe colors of Nick Bantock Stamp Pads on the Craft Sheet. Pick up colors with the Waterbrush to color in stamped image. • 3. Turn the Melting Pot to the UTEE setting. Pour in chosen color of UTEE Brightz. Place lid on to completely melt. • 4. Sandwich stamped image between two pieces of Memory Glass. • 5. Holding the top of the Memory Glass, dip into the melted UTEE in the Melting Pot. "Dredge" the glass through the Melting Pot to get it to push up and cover unstamped area of the memory glass. • 6. Place onto the Craft Sheet and immediately stamp Floral Border into the warm UTEE. Allow to cool. • 7. Pull off the rubber stamp. • 8. Shake up Silver Metallic Mixatives and squirt some onto the Craft Sheet. With your finger, pick up some ink and lightly rub onto the high points of the stamped UTEE. • 9. Dip opposite end of glass into melted UTEE to create a small UTEE border. • 10. Place on pin back.

Shy Eye Pin: Follow directions 1-8. • 9. Place Glossy Accents on the bottom portion of the UTEE stamped image. • 10. Dip Glossy Accented area into BeaDazzles. Let Dry. • 11. Place pin back on back.

Tips and Techniques

1. Rather than dipping one side, just dip all four sides for a "faux soldered" look.

2. Add *UTEE Flex* to melted *UTEE* in the *Melting Pot* when more strength is needed in your Melt Art.

1. Stamp image onto trimmed paper.

2. Rub ink onto *Craft Sheet* and color image with a waterbrush.

3. Melt *UTEE* in a *Melting Pot* (Violet, Fuchsia or Lime).

4. Sandwich image between *Memory Glass.*

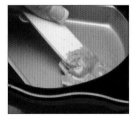

5. Dip *Memory Glass* into melted *UTEE.*

6. Stamp image onto melted *UTEE.* Let Dry.

Floral Pin: Rub *Metallic Mixatives* on stamped image.

Shy Eye Pin: Add *Glossy Accents* to stamped area.

Dip into *BeaDazzles.*

Attach pin to piece with *Glossy Accents.*

Adirondack Embossing Powder

Adirondack Marbled Keepsake Box

by Robin Beam

This is the perfect box with a masculine look created using the Adirondack earth tone palette.

SIZE: 4½" x 4½" x 2¾" tall

MATERIALS: *Ranger Adirondack* Embossing Powders - Bottle, Butterscotch, Cranberry, Denim, Eggplant, Terra Cotta • *Tim Holtz Adirondack Color Wash* - Bottle, Butterscotch, Cranberry, Denim, Eggplant, Terra Cotta • *Heatit* Craft Tool • *Inkssentials Non-Stick Craft Sheet* • *Cut n' Dry Foam* • Clear *Ultra Thick Embossing Enamel/UTEE* • *Melting Pot* • *Melt Art Kool Toolz*

SUPPLIES: Wooden box with inlay lid • Scissors • Tweezers • Toothpick

INSTRUCTIONS:

1. On the Craft Sheet, shake out lines of Embossing Powders so they are butted up against one another, to a 3-4" square. • 2. Turn on the Heatit Tool and starting with it held higher, allow the Embossing Powders to start to melt. As it melts, continue to move the Heatit Tool closer. 3. Once the entire area is melted through (make sure it's not just melted on the surface), move the Heatit Tool up higher and begin to run the wire or toothpick up and down in one direction. • 4. Keeping the Embossing Powder warm with the Heatit Tool, begin to run a toothpick in the opposite direction. See how the powders are pulled and are beginning to marble? Keep doing this until the desired look is maintained. Do not marble too much as it will begin to look muddied. Allow to cool. • 5. While still warm and able to be picked up, peel the marbled sheet from the Craft Sheet. Cut into squares. Option: cut into random pieces to look more like broken tile. • 6. Figure out the basic layout of the tiles and how they will fit in the inlay box lid. • 7. Turn the Melting Pot on to the UTEE setting and pour in Clear UTEE. Place lid on and allow to melt. • 8. While the UTEE is melting, spray desired colors of Color Wash onto the Craft Sheet. With a square of foam, pick up color and apply to wood area. Repeat and use different square of foam for each color. • 9. Use Heatit Tool to dry and heat set ink. • 10. Once UTEE is fully melted, pour into the inlay box lid until it almost reaches the top. 11. Quickly work and place the marble "tiles" in place in the box lid. • 12. Once placed, use Heatit Tool to remelt top so that the marbled powder tiles melt flush into the UTEE. Let cool.

Tips and Techniques

1. Because *Adirondack* Embossing Powders are created with a white resin core and coated with color, when you run the wire through the warm, melted powder, the white core starts to show through as well as pulling into the other colors causing it to "marbleize".

2. Emboss the *Adirondack* Embossing Powder in small batches; otherwise, you will not be able to keep it warm enough at one time to marble.

3. It is best to keep the *Heatit* Tool 1"- 2" away from the surface. If there is not enough air able to flow through the heat tool, like with other heat appliances, it will shut off as a safety feature, but not turn back on again.

4. Do not stir melting *UTEE* as it will end up with bubbles in your work.

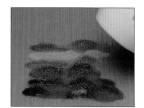

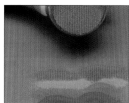

1. Shake out lines of embossing powder next to each other.

2. Heat powder to fuse a layer together.

3. Run a craft pick through the warm powder. Let Dry.

4. Cut warm, but hardened powder into squares.

1. Stamp four fern images on cardstock.

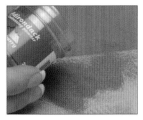

2. Sprinkle embossing powder over images.

3. Emboss with a *Heatit* tool.

4. Mix one scoop of each powder into one container.

5. Stamp a large fern and add embossing mixture.

6. Tap off the excess and emboss image with the *Heatit* tool.

7. Cut out embossed images.

See Everything Fern Card

by Robin Beam

Show off the beauty of Adirondack Embossing Powders. These powders are a unique consistency of grains of white resin coated in colors. Thus, when mixed together, each grain of color remains separate when embossed.

SIZE: 7" x 8½"

MATERIALS: *Ranger Adirondack* Embossing Powders - Bottle, Butterscotch, Cranberry, Denim, Eggplant, Espresso, Ginger • Walnut Stain *Tim Holtz Distress* Ink pad • Sepia *Archival* Ink pad • *Inkssentials Non-Stick Craft Sheet* • *Big & Bossy* Clear Embossing Pad • *Heatit* Craft Tool • *Cut n' Dry Foam*

SUPPLIES: Rubber stamps (*Club Scrap* Unmounted Borders and Backgrounds) • Mixing cup • Spoon • 8½" x 11" cardstock (2 Desert Storm, 1 Brown) • Glue stick • Scissors

INSTRUCTIONS:

1. On 2" x 8" Desert Storm cardstock, stamp small fern stamp using Clear Embossing Pad. • 2. Sprinkle on Cranberry Embossing Powder. Shake off excess and return to jar. • 3. Repeat steps 1-2 for remaining colors of Embossing Powders on supply list. • 4. Using spoon, place equal parts of each color of Adirondack Embossing Powders into a cup and stir until powders are evenly mixed. • 5. Emboss large fern stamp 3 times on 4" x 5" Desert Storm cardstock with Clear embossing ink and Embossing Powder Mixture. 6. Cut out the small embossed images ⅞" x 1½" and the large ones 1⅜" x 3". • 7. On 5½" x 8½" Desert Storm cardstock, stamp small fern in a block design using Sepia ink. • 8. Cut Brown cardstock base 7" x 8½". • 9. Glue stamped cardstock to Brown base, leaving a 1" border on the bottom. Stamp "see everything" centered on the bottom portion of the Brown base with Distress Ink. • 10. Rip Brown cardstock strips ¾" x 8½" and 1" x 8½". Rip each side of the strip toward you for a more textured look along the edges. • 11. Using a square of foam, edge ripped strips with Distress Ink. • 12. Glue wider strip to the top third of the stamped cardstock and the thinner strip to the section below it. • 13. Glue small ferns in place centered over the bottom ripped strip of cardstock. Alternate the direction of the fern images. 14. Adhere large fern images.

Tips and Techniques

1. Some of the following color combinations make wonderful seasonal cards.

Bottle and Cranberry: Holiday

Cranberry, Ginger, Espresso, Bottle and Butterscotch: Autumn

2. When stamping with an unmounted rubber stamp on an acrylic block, placement of the stamp is easy since you can see where the stamp is being placed.

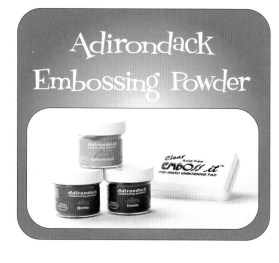

Adirondack Embossing Powder

Adirondack Clover Card
by Debbie Tlach

SIZE: 4" x 4½"
MATERIALS: *Ranger Adirondack* Embossing Powders - Bottle, Butterscotch, Denim, Eggplant, Espresso • *Heatit* Craft Tool • *Emboss It* Clear Embossing Pad • *Popit! Shapes* ⅛" Squares • *Melt Art Kool Toolz* tweezers/spoon
SUPPLIES: Rubber stamp (*Fred B. Mullet* Big Clover Group) • Cardstock (Desert Storm, Purple, Black) • Glue stick • Craft knife • Scissors • Cups to hold Embossing Powder mixes

Tips and Techniques
The mixed powders shaken off the clover image can be saved in another container, creating yet another mix.

INSTRUCTIONS:
1. Mix into a cup or container 1 scoop of Bottle and a ½ scoop of Butterscotch Embossing Powders (Mix A) with the spoon end of the Kool Toolz Tweezers. • 2. In another container mix 1 scoop Bottle and 1 scoop Denim Embossing Powders (Mix B). • 3. In third container mix 1 scoop Eggplant and 1 scoop Espresso Embossing Powders (Mix C). • 4. Ink up clover stamp with the Emboss It Pad. Stamp onto Desert Storm cardstock. • 5. Shake a small amount of the various Embossing Powder combinations onto the appropriate areas of the stamped image. Mix A was used on the stems, Mix B on the leaves and Mix C on the clover.
6. Tap excess Embossing Powder off.
7. Heat emboss with the Heatit Tool.
8. Cut around the image and set aside. • 9. Mix 1 scoop of each of the Embossing Powders listed in the supplies list into another container.
10. Cut Black cardstock into a 3½" square. Apply ink to the adjacent 2 edges of the square with the Emboss it Pad using the stamp pad directly to the paper. • 11. Pour the powder mix over the inked paper.
12. Carefully tap off excess and return to the cup. • 13. Heat emboss with Heatit Tool. Overlay smaller piece of black cardstock to create Adirondack 'speckled' corner border.
14. Cut, layer and glue the card together, using Popit! Shapes under the clover group image.

1. Mix 1 scoop of Butterscotch and ½ scoop of Bottle.

2. Mix 1 scoop each of Denim and Bottle together.

3. Mix 1 scoop each of Eggplant and Espresso together.

4. Ink stamp.

5. Stamp image onto cardstock.

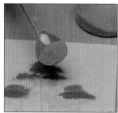

6. Sprinkle mixtures onto desired areas.

7. Emboss image with a *Heatit* tool.

8. Cut out image.

9. Mix one scoop of each embossing powder into a separate container.

10. Ink two edges of cardstock.

11. Spread new mixture onto inked area.

12. Emboss inks with a *Heatit* tool.

Coloring with Perfect Pearls

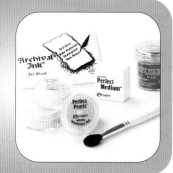

Take Wing Card

by Julia Andrus

SIZE: 5" x 7"

MATERIALS: *Ranger Perfect Pearls* Pigment Kit - Pastel • *Perfect Ink Refresher* • Mountain Meadow *Big & Juicy* Rainbow Pad • Water Mister

SUPPLIES: Rubber stamps (*Judikins* Fiery Campylotes Butterfly; *Jade Stamps* Brushed Alphabet upper and lower case) • *Prism Papers* cardstock (7" x 10" Island Mist Medium, 4½" x 6½" Island Mist Dark, 4" x 6" Razzleberry Medium, 4" x 6", 4" x 6" Midnight Black) • Brads • *Xyron Wishblade* "Take Wing" die cut • Glue stick • Silk ribbon ¼" wide • Small mixing cups • Craft sticks or mixing spoons • Water

INSTRUCTIONS:

Water Webbing Paper Technique:

1. Ink Butterfly and "fly" stamps with Mountain Meadow Big & Juicy Pad. • 2. Stamp images on Chalk Cardstock. 3. Immediately spray stamped image with water and spray right onto the image to make the ink bleed. Option: manipulate the paper to make more webbing. • 4. Dust image with Perfect Pearls Pigment powders before the piece is dry, but not too wet or it will just paint the surface. • 5. Cut Butterfly image in half and cut into two matching size rectangles. Layer onto Razzleberry cardstock.

Northern Lights Paper Technique:

6. Mix several colors of Perfect Pearls Pigment powders in cups or paint palette to form creamy paints. • 7. Spray Black cardstock with Perfect Ink Refresher and rub into the paper surface with a paper towel. 8. QUICKLY dab the paints over the paper with a paintbrush. • 9. Mist with water and manipulate the paper to make the colors bleed and run. • 10. Let

dry. • 11. Rip one side of the paper toward you (so there is a rough Black edge showing).

Assembly:

12. Cut "Take Wing" phrase with Wishblade out of the Razzleberry cardstock. • 13. Assemble by layering the Northern Lights Paper onto Island Mist Dark and then onto Island Mist Medium folded card. • 14. Attach Butterfly images lined up, but slightly apart and "askew" with ribbon glued beneath the top half of the butterfly. • 15. Use Brad to Attach "fly" cardstock. • 16. Glue on "Take Wing" die cut.

Water Webbing

1. Stamp image onto cardstock.

2. Mist image with water.

3. Add *Perfect Pearls* to misted image.

4. Cut image in half.

Northern Lights

5. Spray cardstock with *Perfect Ink Refresher*.

6. Pick up *Perfect Pearls* Powder with a waterbrush.

7. Quickly paint random lines onto cardstock.

8. Mist cardstock with water.

1. Rub *Perfect Medium* over one corner of cardstock.

2. Brush on *Perfect Pearls* over inked area.

3. Ink a stamp and press into powder to lift off the powder.

Tips and Techniques

When lifting, if using the same stamp more than once, be sure to clean it and restamp with *Perfect Medium* each time to assure a clean lifting of *Perfect Pearls* from the surface.

Dusted and Lifted Autumn Leaves

by Robin Beam, technique by Julia Andrus

Create positive and negative images with the magic of Perfect Pearls and Perfect Medium.

SIZE: 5" x 8½"

MATERIALS: *Ranger Perfect Pearls* Pigment Kits: Naturals - Kiwi, Rust, Plum, Blue Smoke; Jewels - Forever Red, Forever Green; Aged Patina - Heirloom Gold, Pewter, Green Patina; Metallics - Perfect Bronze, Perfect Copper • Clear *Perfect Medium* Pad • *Perfect Brushes*

SUPPLIES: Rubber stamps (*Fred B. Mullet* Silver Birch, Turkey Oak Leaf, London Plane, Paper Birch, Spring Cherry; *Stampers Anonymous - Tim Holtz* Sometimes) • Black matte cardstock • Scrap Paper

INSTRUCTIONS:
1. Cut Black cardstock 8½" x 10". Fold to 5" x 8½". • 2. Rip a piece of scrap paper and mask the left ⅔ of the cardstock. • 3. Rub an even coverage of Perfect Medium Pad direct to paper over exposed area. Remove scrap paper mask. • 4. On left side of cardstock, stamp various leaf images inked with Perfect Medium. • 5. Using detail brush, pick up different colors of Perfect Pearls Pigment powders and dust the leaves and solid area that was coated with Perfect Medium. • 6. Remove excess pigment powders with larger whisk brush. • 7. Stamp "Sometimes" stamp with Perfect Medium into solid Perfect Pearls covered area of card. When you remove the stamp, the Perfect Medium on the stamp "lifted" the Perfect Pearls from the surface, creating a "negative" stamped image. • 8. Repeat this technique with some of the leaf stamps on the right edge of the card. • 9. Lightly mist with water to further "fix" the Perfect Pearls. Let dry.

Lifting Off Perfect Pearls with an Inked Rubber Stamp

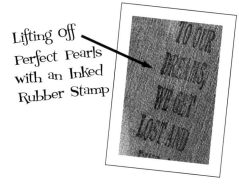

Apply Perfect Pearls to a Stamped Image

Pearlized Fish Card

by Bonnie Egenton, technique by Julia Andrus
Rather than creating a watercolor effect with just water, create a beautiful, pearlized watercolor effect with Perfect Pearls paint.

SIZE: 4¼" x 5½"

MATERIALS: *Ranger Perfect Pearls* Pigment Kit - Metallic: Perfect Pearl • Black *Perfect Medium* Pad • *Perfect Brushes* • *Inkssentials Non-Stick Craft Sheet* • Black Embossing Powder • *Heatit* Craft Tool • *Tim Holtz Distress* Ink pad - Peeled Paint, Scattered Straw) • Jet Black *Archival* Ink pad • *Cut n' Dry Foam*

SUPPLIES: Rubber stamps (*Magenta* Netting; *Impression Obsession* Fish Stained Glass) • Watercolor Pencils • Cardstock (White matte, Sage, Yellow) • *AccuCut* Die cuts (A2 Card, Mat-Circle)

INSTRUCTIONS:
1. Ink fish stamp with Black Perfect Medium Pad. • 2. Stamp image on White matte cardstock. • 3. Sprinkle on Embossing Powder; pour off excess back into the jar. • 4. Emboss image with Heatit Tool. • 5. Color in image with watercolor pencils. • 6. Make pearlized paint with Perfect Pearls powder. Add enough water to create a translucent paint. • 7. Wet watercolored image with Perfect Pearls paint mixture. • 8. Allow to dry - what a wonderful, pearly effect.
9. Cut out fish image and set aside. • 10. Using AccuCut machine, cut circle card in Yellow cardstock and cut layering circle in Sage cardstock. Glue Sage cardstock to front of Yellow card. • 11. On a piece of Yellow scrap cardstock, stamp netting image in Scattered Straw Distress Ink. Overstamp phrase stamp with Jet Black ink.
12. Rip around edges of stamped image. Using foam to apply ink, softly shade edges with Peeled Paint Distress Ink. • 13. Adhere to card front below circle opening. • 14. Shade edges of card with Peeled Paint Distress Ink. • 15. Adhere fish image to inside of card, lining up with circle opening.

1. Color embossed image with colored pencils. **2.** Pick up *Perfect Pearls* powder with a waterbrush. **3.** Paint penciled image with the waterbrush.

Pearlized Spring Card

by Bonnie Egenton, technique by Julia Andrus

SIZE: 5⅜" x 8½"

MATERIALS: *Ranger Perfect Pearls* Metallic Pigment Kit - Perfect Pearl • Black *Perfect Medium* Pad • *Perfect Brushes* • *Inkssentials Non-Stick Craft Sheet* • Black Embossing Powder • *Heatit* Craft Tool • Jet Black *Archival* Ink pad • *Cut n' Dry Foam* • *Paper Creaser* bone folder

SUPPLIES: Rubber stamps (*Hero Arts* Seasonal Memories; *Magenta* Spring Flowers Trio) • Watercolor Pencils • Cardstock (White matte, Purple, Green, Orchid) • Glue stick • *Junkitz - Tim Holtz Metalz* Photo Anchorz • ¹⁄₁₆" hole punch • Brads

INSTRUCTIONS:
1. Ink floral stamp with Black Perfect Medium Pad. • 2. Stamp image on White matte cardstock. • 3. Sprinkle on Black Embossing Powder; pour off excess back into the jar. • 4. Emboss image with Heatit Tool. 5. Color in image with watercolor pencils. • 6. Make pearlized paint with Perfect Pearls powder. Add enough water to create a translucent paint. • 7. Wet watercolored image with Perfect Pearls paint mixture. • 8. Add spots of pearlized color by dipping brush in watery paint and tapping over image. • 9. You may not see the pearlized effect right away. Let it dry and voila! - what a wonderful, pearly look to your watercolors. • 10. Trim around image. Layer to Orchid cardstock to create a frame. • 11. Make holes with hole punch in each

Tips and Techniques

1. Open line image rubber stamps work best for this technique.

2. Embossing with Black ink and Black Embossing Powder will create the most opaque embossed image.

3. Instead of using a cup of water and a paintbrush, use a waterbrush to create the paint, easily using the *Craft Sheet* as your palette.

4. The *Craft Sheet* cleans up easily with a paper towel and water.

corner of the Orchid cardstock. Place Photo Anchorz in each with a brad to hold it in place. • 12. Cut Purple cardstock to a 6⅜" x 6⅝". Fold to 3⅜" x 6⅜" with a bone folder. Adhere stamped flowers to Purple card. • 13. Create a background with Green cardstock. Stamp phrase seven times in a grid pattern using Jet Black ink pad. Adhere Purple card to center of Green background.

1. Cut cardstock to size.

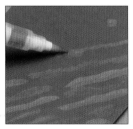

2. Spray cardstock with *Perfect Ink Refresher*.

3. Work *Ink Refresher* into cardstock with a paper towel.

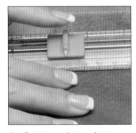

4. Pick up *Perfect Pearls* Powder with a waterbrush.

5. Quickly paint random lines onto cardstock.

6. Mist cardstock with water.

7. Stamp image onto cardstock.

8. Mist image with water.

9. Add *Perfect Pearls* to misted image.

Ancient Motif Card

by Julia Andrus

SIZE: 6" x 6"

MATERIALS: *Ranger Perfect Pearls* Pigment Kits: Metallics Perfect Copper; Naturals - Kiwi, Plum, Blue Smoke • Spice *Big & Juicy* Rainbow Pad • *Perfect Ink Refresher* • Water Mister

SUPPLIES: Rubber stamp (*JudiKins* Small Tribal Square Flower) • *Prism Papers* cardstock (Chocolate, White Tan, 6" x 6" Chocolate card) • Small mixing cups • Water • Craft Sticks or mixing spoons • Paper towel • Photo Corners die cut

INSTRUCTIONS:

Northern Lights Paper Technique:

1. Mix several colors of Perfect Pearls Pigment powders in cups or paint palette to form creamy paints.
2. Spray Chocolate cardstock with Perfect Ink Refresher and rub into the paper surface with a paper towel. • 3. QUICKLY dab the paints over the paper with a paintbrush. • 4. Mist with water and manipulate the paper to make the colors bleed and run. • 5. Let dry.
6. Cut to 5¾" x 5¾" panel. Save a 1" strip of the Northern Lights Paper and die cut the photo corners.

Water Webbing Paper Technique:

7. Ink Tribal Square Flower Stamp with Big & Juicy Rainbow Pad and stamp on White Tan cardstock.
8. Immediately spray stamped image with water-spray right onto the image to make the ink bleed. Manipulate the paper to make more webbing if desired. • 9. Dust image with Perfect Pearls Pigment powder before the image is dry, but not too wet or will just paint surface.

Glimmer Paper Technique and Assembly:

10. Create a creamy paint by mixing Kiwi Perfect Pearls with water in a small cup. • 11. Paint Kiwi onto Chocolate cardstock and quickly buff off with a paper towel. 12. Assemble card and adhere Northern Lights Photo Corners with glue stick onto the stamped image.

Coloring with Perfect Pearls

Pearled Seashell Card

by Bonnie Egenton,
technique by Julia Andrus

SIZE: 5½" x 6¾"

MATERIALS: *Ranger Perfect Pearls* Metallic Pigment Kit - Perfect Pearl • Black *Perfect Medium* Pad • *Perfect Brushes* • *Inkssentials Non-Stick Craft Sheet* • Black Embossing Powder • *Heatit* Craft Tool • *Adirondack:* Alcohol Inks - Eggplant, Wild Plum; Alcohol Ink Applicator; Replacement Felt; Wild Plum Dye Ink Pad • Walnut Stain *Tim Holtz Distress* Ink pad • Jet Black *Archival* Ink pad • *Cut n' Dry Foam*

SUPPLIES: Rubber stamps (*Artful Stamper* Shells; *Stampers Anonymous* Endless Journey) • *Junkitz - Tim Holtz Mini Platez* • ¹⁄₁₆" hole punch • Watercolor pencils • Cardstock (White matte, Black, Kraft) • Glue stick

INSTRUCTIONS:

1. Ink the shell stamp with Black Perfect Medium Pad. • 2. Stamp image on White cardstock. • 3. Sprinkle on Black Embossing Powder; pour excess back into the jar. • 4. Emboss image with Heatit Tool. • 5. Color in image with watercolor pencils. • 6. Make pearlized paint with Perfect Pearls Pigment powder. Add enough water to create a translucent paint. • 7. Wet watercolor pencil image with Perfect Pearls paint mixture. 8. Add spots of pearlized color by dipping brush in watery paint and tapping brush over image. • 9. You may not see the pearlized effect right away. Let it dry and voila! - what a wonderful, pearly look to your watercolors.
10. Trim around image. Layer to Black cardstock to create a frame. Set aside.
11. Create a card with Kraft cardstock. Stamp phrase in Jet Black ink at the bottom of the front of card. • 12. Stamp phrase again on White scrap piece. Cut out "scenic route" to fit the Mini Platez.
13. Apply a drop of Wild Plum and Eggplant Alcohol Ink to Felt on Ink Applicator. Colorize Metal Platez and allow to dry. • 14. Punch holes to place Mini Platez and adhere with brads. Secure phrase inside the Mini Platez.
15. Using small piece of foam, distress edges of card in Adirondack Wild Plum and Distress Walnut Stain to give it an antique effect. 16. Adhere pearlized Shells to front of card.

Sun Card

by Julia Andrus

SIZE: 4⅞" x 6⅝"

MATERIALS: *Ranger Perfect Pearls* Naturals Pigment Kits - Pastel, Kiwi • *Perfect Ink Refresher* • *Perfect Medium* • *Embossing Antiquities* Terra Cotta • Mountain Meadow *Big & Juicy* Rainbow Pad • Water Mister • *Heatit* Craft Tool

SUPPLIES: Rubber stamps (Sun, *Hero Arts* Florentine Scroll Background) • Cardstock (7" x 10" Royal Blue, Chili for Northern Lights Background Paper and card panel; Oxford White) • *Sizzix* Die Cuts (Filigree Clock, Buckles Charms) • Small mixing cups • Craft sticks or mixing spoons • Satin Ribbon, ¼" wide • Tiny tag • Fiber • Paper towels

INSTRUCTIONS:

Water Webbing Paper Technique:

1. Ink Florentine Scroll background stamp with Big & Juicy Rainbow Pad and stamp on White cardstock. • 2. Immediately spray stamped image with water. Spray right onto the image to make the ink bleed. Manipulate the paper to make more webbing. • 3. Dust image with Sunflower Sparkle (Pastels) Pigment Powder before the image is dry, but not too wet or will just paint the surface.

Northern Lights Paper Technique:

4. Mix several colors of Perfect Pearls Pigment powders in cups or paint palette to form creamy paints. • 5. Spray Chili cardstock with Perfect Ink Refresher and rub into the paper surface with a paper towel. •6. QUICKLY dab the paints over the paper with a paintbrush. • 7. Mist with water and manipulate the paper to make the colors bleed and run. • 8. Let dry.

Hammered Faux Perfect Metal Hardware Technique:

9. Die cut 3-5 of the buckle image. • 10. Adhere layers of paper together with glue stick. 11. Rub Perfect Medium Pad onto top layer of tabs. • 12. Using Detail Perfect Brush, pick up chosen colors of Perfect Pearls Pigment powders and dust onto die cuts. • 13. Brush off excess pigment powders with larger whisk Perfect Brush. • 14. Mist with water. This will activate the binders in the Perfect Pearls and soften the paper for the next step. • 15. Using the dull end of either Perfect Brush, dent the die cuts to create the hammered effect. 16. Option: brush on additional Perfect Pearls for a brighter look. For an even more distressed look, edge hammered die cuts with sandpaper or sanding block.

Assembly:

17. Ink Sun stamp with Perfect Medium and stamp onto White cardstock. • 18. Sprinkle on Terra Cotta Embossing Powder; tap off excess and return to jar. • 19. Emboss with Heatit Tool and cut out. • 20. Die Cut Filigree Clock from cardstock and layer Sun over it.
21. Assemble.

you brighten my day

If you do nothing unexpected, nothing unexpected ever happens.

be yourself

good thoughts to you • good thoughts to you

Painting with Perfect Pearls

Painting with Perfect Pearls
by Robin Beam

GENERAL MATERIALS: *Ranger Perfect Pearls* Pigment Powders • *Perfect Medium* Pad • Embossing Powders - Clear, Liquid Platinum, Queen's Gold • *Inkssentials Non-Stick Craft Sheet* • *Heatit* Craft Tool

SUPPLIES: Rubber stamps (Line image with open area - see instructions below for specific rubber stamps for each project)• *Niji* Waterbrush • Water • Black cardstock

GENERAL INSTRUCTIONS:
1. Ink a rubber stamp with Perfect Medium Pad - this medium has a long open time so it makes the "perfect" embossing ink. • 2. Stamp inked image on cardstock. • 3. Sprinkle on chosen Embossing Powder; shake off excess and place back in jar.
4. Emboss image with Heatit Tool; set aside.
5. Since you are creating a number of paints, use the Craft Sheet as your palette. • 6. Use a wet brush to pick up some Perfect Pearls Pigment powder. Mix into a paint on the Craft Sheet. To make a more opaque paint, use less water; to make more translucent, add more water. • 7. Paint in the image. Think of it as a stained glass image.
8. To create tones of color, add Interference colors for some "pop". To tone down an image, add in some of the new Aged Patina colors. To lighten a color, add the Perfect Pearls Pigment powder from the Metallic palette. • 9. If using a waterbrush, just squeeze it into a paper or cloth towel to clean before using a new color. • 10. When the paint is dry, it's fixed to the surface. • 11. Layer onto card or incorporate into your scrapbooking.

Tips and Techniques
As an alternative to embossing, use a metallic outline sticker, then paint *Perfect Pearls* between the design to look like Cloisonne.

Strawberries Card - SIZE: 5⅞" x 6"
Rubber stamps (*Peddler's Pack Stampworks* Strawberry Background; *Hero Arts* Pocketful o' Kind Words)
Unexpected Card - SIZE: 5½" x 6"
Rubber stamps (*Stampers Anonymous* Be Yourself Ticket Background; *Paperbag Studios* Unexpected)
4 Kitties Card - SIZE: 5" x 6¼"
Rubber stamps (*Hero Arts* Cat Portraits, Wavy Wishes)

1. Stamp image, add powder and heat set.

2. Use a water brush to mix *Perfect Pearls* into a paint.

3. Paint image with *Perfect Pearls* mixture.

Sticky Note Book Holders
'Out of the Desert'
by Julia Andrus

SIZE: 3⅛" x 3⅛"

MATERIALS: *Ranger Perfect Pearls* Pigment Kits: Metallics - Perfect Copper, Perfect Bronze; Aged Patina - Green Patina, Heirloom Gold, Blue Patina • *Perfect Medium* Pad • *Perfect Brushes* • *Perfect Ink Refresher* • *Heatit* Craft Tool • *Tim Holtz Distress* Ink pads • Water Mister

SUPPLIES: Rubber stamp (*Magenta*) • Cardstock (*Prism Papers* Midnight Black for hardware, Sandpaper for cover, Nordic Blue for Blue panel) • Sticky Back note paper • Paper towels or foam brush • Brads • Die Cuts (*AccuCut* 3-D Sticky Notes Holder Long Cut; *Sizzix* Buckles Charms, Sizzlits strips)

INSTRUCTIONS:

Faux Leather Paper Technique:
1. Spray both sides of Sandpaper cardstock with Perfect Ink Refresher. • 2. Work into paper with paper towels or foam brush. Paper will become supple and more bendable after applying Perfect Ink Refresher. • 3. Gently crumple the paper. The more crumpled, the finer the texture. Unfold. • 4. Lightly brush Perfect Pearls Pigment powders over one side of the crumpled paper. • 5. Dry by ironing or using a Heatit Tool. 6. After drying, the paper will be soft and is ideal to cover boxes and book covers. The paper can be mitered without breaking. • 7. Die Cut Sticky Notes Holder and Sizzlits Strip (to form the strap for the cover) from the finished cardstock.

Hammered Perfect Faux Metal Hardware Technique:
8. Die cut 3-5 of the chosen buckle. • 9. Adhere layers of paper together with glue stick. • 10. Rub Perfect Medium Pad onto top layer of buckle. • 11. Using detail Perfect Brush, pick up chosen colors of Perfect Pearls Pigment powders and dust onto die cut. • 12. Brush off excess pigment powders with large brush. • 13. Mist with water. This will activate the binders in the Perfect Pearls and soften the paper for the next step. 14. Using the dull end of a Perfect Brush, dent die cuts to create a hammered effect. • 15. Brush on additional Perfect Pearls for a brighter look. For an even more distressed look, edge hammered die cuts with sandpaper or sanding block. • 16. Place chosen collage image in tag circle and attach to cover or stamp image on cover with Distress Ink pad. • 17. Attach brads to finished hardware; tie ribbon around book and attach hardware or attach leather strap around the book with the buckle.

'Vintage Hardware'

SIZE: 3⅛" x 3⅛"

MATERIALS: *Ranger Perfect Pearls* Pigment Kit - Aged Patina • *Perfect Ink Refresher* • *Heatit* Craft Tool

SUPPLIES: Cardstock (*Prism Papers* Midnight Black for Hardware and Cover, Suede Brown Medium for Torn Edge Piece) • Sticky Back Note Pad • ¼" wide ribbon • Collage Sheet • Brads • Tacky Adhesive • Die cuts (*AccuCut* 3-D Sticky Notes Holder Long Cut, Gift Tag-Circle & Band; *Sizzix* Hinges, Latches, Handle & Photo Turns, Locks)

Tips and Techniques

The Faux Leather Paper process can be performed on both light and dark colored papers. If using light colored paper, you can use chalk or ink to highlight the paper along with *Perfect Pearls*.

1. Spray cardstock with *Perfect Ink Refresher*.

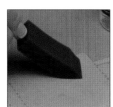

2. Work Refresher into paper with foam brush.

3. Gently crumple paper.

4. Lightly brush *Perfect Pearls* over crumpled paper.

5. Dry with *Heatit* tool or iron.

6. Die-cut multiple buckles for layering.

7. Adhere layers of buckles together.

8. Rub *Perfect Medium* over the buckle.

9. Dust *Perfect Pearls* over the buckle.

10. Mist buckle with water.

11. Dent buckle with end of paintbrush.

12. Bend to shape the handle.

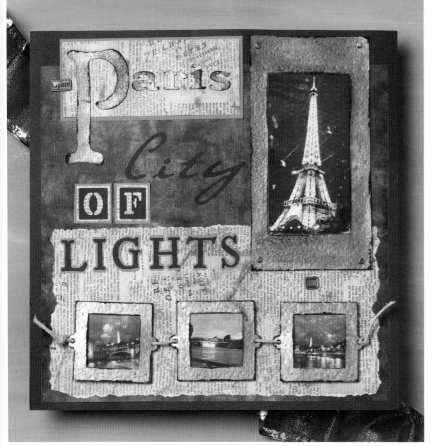

'Paris City of Lights' Scrapbook Page

by Julia Andrus

SIZE: 12" x 12"
MATERIALS: *Ranger Perfect Pearls* Pigment Kits:
Aged Patina - Pewter, Blue Patina; Metallics -
Perfect Pearl • *Tim Holtz Distress* Ink pad • *Cut n'
Dry* Foam
SUPPLIES: 12" x 12" cardstock (*Prism Papers*
Midnight Black for frames and "Paris" letters,
Twilight Dark for background, Twilight Medium
for "Paris" mat and outline for other letters) •
Papers (Book Print, Plum Texture) • Brads
(Round, Word) • Twine
• *Xyron* (Font; Photo Frames; Wishblade)
INSTRUCTIONS:
1. Cut Plum Texture Scrapbook Paper to make a
panel and layer onto the Midnight Blue Cardstock.
2. Tear Book Print Scrapbook Paper. Ink square of
foam and rub across Distress Ink pad. Ink edges of
paper. Repeat process for "City of Lights" part of
Paris title.
Hammered Perfect Faux Metal Hardware:
3. Using the Wishblade, die cut three small frames
and one large frame. For each frame cut the image
3-5 times, depending on how thick you want the
frames to look. • 4. Follow the instructions on
page 35. • 5. Repeat the Hammered Perfect Faux
Metal process with the letters spelling "Paris", but
use only one layer of paper.
Finish: 6. String the small frames together with
twine and insert decorative brads.
7. Adhere "Paris" letters and frames as shown.

Tips and Techniques

Instead of using the back of the *Perfect Brushes* to create the hammered effect, fashion your own hammering mallet. Hammer small, round-head linoleum nails into one side of a rubber mallet and you're ready to create hammered metal out of paper.

'Alisha' Scrapbook Page

by Julia Andrus

SIZE: 12" x 12"
MATERIALS: *Ranger Perfect Pearls* Pigment Kits -
Aged Patina; Naturals: Kiwi • *Tim Holtz Distress* Ink
pads • *Cut n' Dry* Foam • Water Mister
SUPPLIES: Rubber stamps (*Toy Box Rubber Stamps*
Journal; *JudiKins* Papyrus Background) • *Sizzix* Tabs,
Rectangle and Triangle die cut • *Pine Cone Press*
Single Pocket Journal • Monogram Embossing Plate
• *American Traditional Designs (*Medium Tile Piercing
Template; Embossing Tool) • *Xyron* Wishblade •
Brads • 12" x 12" cardstock (*Prism Papers* White, Tan,
Midnight Black) • Hardware paper • Embossed panels
• Letters • 14" ribbon • Glue stick • Buttons • Paper
towels • Sandpaper or *PM Designs* Scrapper's Block
INSTRUCTIONS:
Pearly Mottled Paper Technique:
1. Ink squares of foam onto Distress Ink pads and
color light cardstock. • 2. Spritz inked paper with
water and blot to create a mottled effect. • 3. Dust
mottled paper with Perfect Pearls Pigment powders.
Because of the binders in Perfect Pearls, when it is
dry, it is fixed; no further fixative is necessary.
4. Overstamp the Perfectly Mottled Paper with
Papyrus stamp inked with Distress Inks.
Hammered Perfect Faux Metal Hardware:
5. Die cut 3-5 of each of the tabs.
6. Follow the instructions on page 35.
Dusting Dry Embossed Tiles:
7. Dry emboss monogram and medium tile templates
on Black cardstock. • 8. Rub surface with Perfect
Medium and dust with Perfect Pearls Pigment powders using Detail Perfect Brush. • 9. Dust off excess
pigment powders with larger, Whisk Perfect Brush.
Library Pocket: 10. Use square of foam to edge
library pocket with Distress Ink. • 11. Stamp Journal
stamp with Distress Ink. • 12. Assemble as in photo.
13. Stitch the dividing lines between hardware tabs.

Stickles & Liquid Pearls

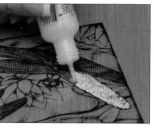

1. Clear the bottle tip by squeezing bottle until all air bubbles are gone.

2. Embellish stamped image with Stickles.

Tips and Techniques

1. Practice with *Stickles* on scrap paper to get flow and to ensure there are no air bubbles.

2. Immediately clean the stamp with *Cleansit* Stamp Cleaner. Because of the "permanency" of the solvent ink, quick clean up is best for your stamps.

Hammered Perfect Faux Metal Hardware

Technique:

• 1. Adhere layers of paper together with glue stick.

• 2. Rub *Perfect Medium* Pad onto top layer of tabs.

• 3. Using Detail Brush, pick up chosen colors of *Perfect Pearls* Pigment powders and dust onto die cuts.

• 4. Brush off excess pigment powders with larger whisk brush.

• 5. Mist with water to activate the binders in the *Perfect Pearls* and soften the paper for the next step.

• 6. Using the dull end of either *Perfect Brush*, dent the die cuts to create the hammered effect.

• 7. Brush on additional *Perfect Pearls* for a brighter look. For an even more distressed look, edge hammered die cuts with sandpaper or sanding block.

'Dragonfly Stained Glass' Glitter Card

by Robin Beam

Stickles is not only the ideal glitter glue for embellishing elements on cards and scrapbook creations, but is also a wonderful and easy way to create a stained glass glitter work of art. No messy, loose glitter to work with.

SIZE: 6¼" x 7½"

MATERIALS: *Ranger Stickles* glitter glue - Lavender, Purple, Star Dust, Goldenrod, Magenta, Eucalyptus, Waterfall, Lime Green • Black *Decor it* ink • *Cut n' Dry Foam* • *Cleansit* Stamp Cleaner • *Perfect Medium* Pad

SUPPLIES: Rubber stamps (*Peddler's Pack Stampworks* Dragonfly Background; *Meer Image Art* Blue Darner Dragonfly) • Transparency • Brads • Mini brads • Light Green cardstock

INSTRUCTIONS:

1. Shake Decor it ink and squeeze out onto a square of foam. Decor it ink is a solvent based pigment ink that works on all porous and non-porous surfaces. • 2. Pat inked foam onto stamp. Be sure to get an even and complete application of ink on rubber stamp. • 3. Stamp image on transparency. Let dry. Note: because this is a solvent based ink it will dry quickly. 4. Begin to "color in" image on the STAMPED side of the image. If possible, work from one side to the other so your hand does not accidentally get into the Stickles. • 5. Place in a safe area and allow to completely dry. • 6. Turn over-see what a beautiful effect the Stickles create. • 7. Cut out Light Green cardstock larger than the transparency. • 8. Stamp Blue Darner Dragonfly with Perfect Medium. It creates a wonderful watermark on the paper. • 9. Cut out transparency to leave a ⅜" border. • 10. Layer onto Green cardstock and use brads to secure.

'I'm Looking Through You' ATC

by Estrella Bianchi

ATCs, or Artist Trading Cards, are all the rage and a fun way to showcase your art on a smaller scale. The use of *Liquid Pearls* and Acrylics pearlized dimensional paint with a detail tip provides a 3-D effect.

ATC SIZE: 2½" x 3½"

MATERIALS: *Ranger* Black *Decor it* ink • *Popit! Shapes* • *Adirondack* Acrylics - Butterscotch, Cranberry, Eggplant, Stream, Wild Plum • *Liquid Pearls* - Baby Blue, Gold Pearl, Lavender Lace, Lemon Yellow, Mint Green, Petal Pink, White Opal • *Cut n' Dry Foam* • *Inkssentials Non-Stick Craft Sheet* • *Cleansit* Stamp Cleaner)

SUPPLIES: Rubber stamps (*Coast Art* Doodle Doll; *Action Instant Printing* Curtains) • 2½" x 3½" ribbed duplex cardstock • Vellum (Heavyweight White, Gold) • #5 brush • Label Maker • Quilling paper • Vellum Tape • Cotton swabs • Detail scissors • Colored pencils • Craft knife • Cutting mat • Glue stick • Black Very Fine Point permanent marker • Glue stick

INSTRUCTIONS:

1. Squeeze out small amounts of Acrylics onto Craft Sheet. With a #5 Brush, paint a randomly colored background on ribbed cardstock. Allow to dry. Clean Craft Sheet with Cleansit. • 2. Shake Black ink, squeeze some onto a square of foam. Stamp Doll image on White vellum. Let dry. Immediately clean stamp with Cleansit. • 3. Turn vellum over, color the back of image with color pencils. • 4. Cut girl out with a knife on a mat, cut out eyes. Stamp Curtain image with Black ink on Gold vellum.
5. Color tassels and fringe from the back of vellum with color pencils. • 6. Cut out curtain. • 7. Pass curtain image through a Xyron Machine using the permanent adhesive cartridge or apply vellum tape to back of curtain image. • 8. Once the acrylic paint is dry, use a Black marker to draw a horizontal line 1¼" up from the bottom of card. • 9. Draw floorboards at an angle to create perspective, then fill floorboards with wood grain. • 10. Adhere curtains on both sides of painted cardstock. Make sure the bottom hem fringe is ⅛" above the bottom edge of card. If necessary, trim the top of curtains so they are even with card. • 11. Attach image with Popit! Shapes. • 12. Punch out words on paper tape using a Label Maker.
13. Color paper tape using pen nibs and Acrylics. Lightly rub the side of pen nib on the paper tape; use several colors this way. • 14. Rub raised surface of letters with Black ink. • 15. Trim paper tape close to the words with detail scissors, then cut words apart. • 16. Adhere pieces of paper tape to card with a glue stick.
17. Add dots with Liquid Pearls or Gold Stickles.

'Queen' ATC

Stickles and Liquid Pearls are not just for "cute" images. They add glamour and that little extra sparkle to vintage and altered art, too.

MATERIALS: *Ranger* Jet Black *Archival* Ink pad • *Stickles* glitter glue - Gold, Starry Night, Lime Green • White Opal *Liquid Pearls*

SUPPLIES: *Peddlers Pack Stampworks* rubber stamp (Miss May) • 2½" x 3½" Black matte cardstock • Scrap of distressed paper • Colored pencils • Glue stick

INSTRUCTIONS:

1. Stamp image on scrapbook paper with Black. • 2. Color in image with pencils, tear into a rectangular shape. • 3. Color the rough, torn edge with color pencils.
4. Adhere stamped image to Black cardstock using a glue stick. • 5. Embellish Crown with Lime Green and Starry Night Stickles and White Opal Liquid Pearls.
6. Create a pattern on Black cardstock by surrounding the image with Gold Stickles.

'Here Comes the Sun' ATC

MATERIALS: *Ranger* Jet Black *Archival* Ink pad • *Popit! Shapes* • *Inkssentials* Non-Stick Craft Sheet • Gold *Stickles* Glitter Glue • *Cut n' Dry Nibs* • Gold *Posh Accent Pen* • *Adirondack:* Pitch Black *Pigment Pen*; Acrylics - Butterscotch, Cranberry, Denim, Lettuce, Pesto

SUPPLIES: Rubber stamp (*Limited Edition Rubber Stamps* Face Close-up) • 2½" x 3½" ribbed Green duplex cardstock • Ivory cardstock • #5 brush • Label Maker • Quilling paper • Glue stick • Colored pencils • Detail scissors

INSTRUCTIONS:

1. Squeeze small amounts of Acrylics onto Craft Sheet. With a #5 Brush, paint a starburst background on ribbed cardstock. Allow to dry. • 2. Stamp Face with Jet Black ink on Ivory cardstock. • 3. Color image with color pencils. • 4. Cut image into a square. Hold square so the blank back is facing you, use a Black Pigment Pen to color the Ivory edges of square. • 5. When acrylic paint is dry, draw rays emanating from the center of card with Gold Posh Pen. • 6. Repeat steps 11 - 17 above.

Tips and Techniques

1. Practice getting a controlled flow of *Liquid Pearls* by squeezing it out on scrap paper first.

2. Sometimes giving *Liquid Pearls* a quick shake down toward the tip first before removing top will push any air bubbles out.

'Happy' Color Wash Scrapbook Page

by Robin Beam

Color Wash is as beautiful on paper as it is on fabric. Create the look of batik using Clear Embossing Powder as a resist with Color Wash for your scrapbooking.

SIZE: 12" x 12"

MATERIALS: *Ranger Tim Holtz Adirondack Color Wash* - Bottle, Butterscotch, Cranberry, Denim, Lettuce, Terra Cotta, Wild Plum • Embossing Powders - Clear, Seafoam White • *Inkssentials Non-Stick Craft Sheet* • *Big & Bossy* Clear Embossing Pad • *Heatit* Craft Tool • 12" x 12" *Gloss Paper* • *Popit! Shapes* ⅛" Squares • Water Mister

SUPPLIES: Rubber stamps (*Hero Arts* Big and Bold Happy, Paisley Prints; *Club Scrap* Big and Tall Upper Case and Lower Case Alphabets) • Black cardstock • Glue stick • Photo

INSTRUCTIONS:

1. On 12" x 12" Gloss Paper, stamp "Happy" stamp with Embossing Ink in lines across the page. Fill in the spaces with the Paisley images.

2. Sprinkle on Clear Embossing Powder. Tap off excess and place back in jar. • 3. Heat emboss with Heatit Tool. • 4. On Craft Sheet, spray Color Wash, placing the colors next to one another and not on top of one another (1-2 pumps per color is good). • 5. Spray the Color Wash "palette" with water. Just a few spritzes will do. You want to help the colors to blend a little. Too much water will lessen the intensity of the color. • 6. Turn the Gloss Paper onto the Craft Sheet GLOSS SIDE DOWN. Press on the paper to ensure that the ink will hit the entire sheet of paper. Carefully turn over and dry the inked paper with the Heatit Tool. Note: don't concentrate the Heatit Tool on one area too long as you do not want to remelt the Embossing Powder.

7. Hint: If there are small areas in the embossed areas that did not fill in with ink, use the Water Mister to "move" the ink to those areas. • 8. For the title, ink Big and Tall Alphabet with Clear Embossing Ink. Note: layout the letters above the area that you are going to be stamping on to make sure that it will fit. • 9. Sprinkle on Seafoam White Embossing Powder. Shake off excess and place back in jar. • 10. Heat emboss with Heatit Tool. • 11. Repeat steps 9-10 for the "Happy" stamp. • 12. Trim paper. • 13. Layer photo onto Black cardstock. Glue down photo and title. • 14. Use Popit! Shapes on the back of the embossed "Happy" image. Place over one of the clear embossed words on the background scrapbook paper.

15. Note: for a scrapbook page like this, less is more. You want to show off the paper that you created.

1. Emboss image onto the background.

2. Spray lines of *Color Wash* next to each other.

3. Mist lines with water.

4. Smoosh background into *Color Wash*.

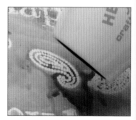

5. Dry with a *Heatit* tool.

INSTRUCTIONS:
1. Over the Craft Sheet, spray Green cardstock with Bottle Color Wash. Let dry. Cut and fold card. 2. Place Floral Mask over dictionary paper and spray with Terra Cotta . Blend with a square of foam. 3. Spray over with Cranberry for a mottled effect. 4. When dictionary paper is dry, remove floral mask. Trim paper to fit to front of card, adhere with glue stick. 5. Punch out image of girl with a 1" circle punch. 6. Cut mica to fit over 1" image. Add both pieces to bottle cap. Fold edges, adhere to card with Glossy Accents. 7. Cut strips of cardstock and run through label maker to make greeting. Ink a square of foam with Stream Stamp Pad, rub over embossed greeting to accentuate. 8. Embellish the flower and around the border of card with Turquoise Stickles.

'Within Me' Masked Color Wash Scrapbook Page

by Erikia Ghumm

Color Wash and Masks are perfect for use on paper as well as fabric.

SIZE: 12" x 12"
MATERIALS: *Ranger Tim Holtz Adirondack Color Wash* - Wild Plum, Butterscotch • *Stickles* Glitter Glue - Aqua, Eucalyptus, Lime Green, Turquoise • *Sea Shells* Dye Ink Stamp Pad - Starfish Green • *Sea Brights* Dye Ink Stamp Pad - Pool • *Cut n' Dry Foam*
SUPPLIES: Rubber stamps (*Heidi Swapp* Flower Patch Mask, Floral Bouquet Large Mask) • Word Stickers • Cardstock • Label Maker • Green acrylic paint • Photo
INSTRUCTIONS:
1. Print or copy a photo onto plain paper. Cut scrap paper to create a mask to place over the original photo. Adhere original photo to background paper. 2. Apply temporary adhesive to back of photo mask. 3. Adhere temporary mask over original photo along with Flower Patch Mask. • 4. Lightly spray with Wild Plum Color Wash. • 5. Blend in wet Color Wash with a cut square of foam. • 6. Spray additional Color Wash to deepen the color. • 7. Reapply the floral mask to another part of the page and repeat until the desired look is achieved. 8. Remove the Flower Patch mask and lightly spray the entire background with Butterscotch Color Wash. • 9. Remove photo mask from the photo and embellish the centers of the flowers with Stickles. • 10. Follow step 7 of Girlfriend Card and color with Starfish Green and Pool inks.

Hey Girlfriend! Card

SIZE: 4½" x 6"
MATERIALS: *Ranger Tim Holtz Adirondack Color Wash* - Bottle, Cranberry, Terra Cotta • *Stickles* Turquoise Glitter Glue • *Adirondack* Dye Ink Stamp Pad - Stream • *Cut n' Dry Foam* • *Inkssentials Non-Stick Craft Sheet* • *Glossy Accents*
SUPPLIES: Rubber stamp (*Heidi Swapp* Floral Bouquet Large Mask) • Cardstock • Label Maker • *Design Originals* Dictionary paper • Green bottle cap • Image of Little Girl • 1" circle punch • Mica • Glue stick

1. Spray page with plum *Color Wash.*

2. Smear *Color Wash* with a piece of *Cut n' Dry Foam.*

3. Respray with plum *Color Wash.*

4. Reposition mask & respray.

5. Spray page with Butterscotch.

6. Remove masks from page.

Adirondack Color Wash on Canvas

Hope, Dream & Love
by Jen Starr
Create glowing colors and sentiments for baby.

SIZE: 8" x 28"

MATERIALS:
Ranger Tim Holtz Adirondack Color Wash - Wild Plum, Butterscotch, Eggplant, Lettuce, Stream, Terra Cotta • *Big & Bossy* Clear Embossing Pad • Clear Embossing Powder • *Heatit* Craft Tool

SUPPLIES: Rubber stamps (*Technique Tuesday* Williamsburg Large Alphabet) • Three 8" x 8" stretched Cotton canvas • Sandpaper • Photos • Clean paper towel • Torn cotton strips

INSTRUCTIONS:
1. Ink words "Hope", "Dream" and "Love" with Clear Embossing Ink.
2. Stamp each word to the top portion of each canvas. Sprinkle on Clear Embossing Powder. Shake off excess and return to jar.
3. Working with one canvas at a time, lightly spritz with water, and then spray enough Color Wash to cover the canvas. Note: do not overlap the colors, but spray them next to one another so they will blend but not get muddy. • 4. Using crumpled paper or cloth towel LIGHTLY dab on the wet canvas to create texture and to help dry canvas. Air dry or speed drying with Heatit Tool; don't concentrate the Heatit Tool on the embossed area for too long as you do not want to remelt the embossed area. • 5. Sandpaper photos lightly around the edges and mount to each canvas. • 6. Attach canvases together with torn fabric by stapling to the back of each canvas.

Tips and Techniques
Dye cloth strips with *Color Wash* to coordinate with canvases. Heat set with *Heatit* Tool before attaching to canvases.

1. Spray canvas with water.

2. Spray canvas with *Color Wash*.

3. Dab canvas with a paper towel.

4. Add Heatit Tool to heat set *Color Wash*.

Family Canvas

by Jen Starr

SIZE: 18" x 24"

MATERIALS: *Ranger Tim Holtz Adirondack Color Wash* - Pesto, Currant, Cranberry, Lettuce, Espresso, Butterscotch) • *Cut n' Dry Foam* • *Glossy Accents* • *Heatit* Craft Tool

SUPPLIES: Stretched canvas (18" x 24", two 8" x 8") • Two 5" x 7" canvas boards • Wood letters • *Fabri-Tac* Glue • Yellow small florals • Buttercup Tastefully Tattered Fabric Strips • Papers (*Basic Grey Jacquard, Gabardine, Mila*) • Photos • *Provo Craft* Carved Wood letters • Sandpaper • White acrylic paint • Copper notions • 3 Silk flowers

INSTRUCTIONS:

1. Spritz large canvas with water; spritz upper left-hand corner with Pesto and Lettuce Color Wash. • 2. Starting from bottom right, spray Cranberry and Currant Color Wash; add more water if necessary to blend colors. • 3. Spritz edges of entire canvas with Espresso Color Wash for a more vintage look. Let dry. • 4. On 8" x 8" canvas, repeat process, spraying first with water, followed by Lettuce and Cranberry Color Wash. Let dry. • 5. Follow the same procedure again on the two canvas boards, spritzing with Butterscotch, Lettuce and Cranberry Color Wash. Let dry. • 6. Cut paper and attach, coordinating paper to the Color Wash colors on the canvas (Gabardine cardstock with the Green side and Jacquard cardstock on the Red side). • 7. Use foam to apply Color Wash to paper edges (match colors to paper). • 8. Cut paper strips from the Mila cardstock to width of 8" x 8" canvas. Glue to edges and distress with foam sprayed with light misting of coordinating Color Wash. Let dry, then attach to larger canvas with Glossy Accents. Note: for added security, staple from the back of the large canvas into the wood frame of the 8" x 8" canvas frames. • 9. Cut length of Fabric Strip and spritz lightly with Lettuce and Butterscotch Color Wash. Dry with Heatit Tool. Attach to canvas. • 10. Lightly spritz fabric flower with Butterscotch Color Wash. Edge flowers with Cranberry Color Wash by spritzing it into a puddle on the Craft Sheet and dipping flower edges into the puddle. Let dry. Attach to canvas with Fabri-Tac Glue. • 11. Attach copper finding in center of flowers with Glossy Accents. • 12. Prime wood letters spelling "Family" with White acrylic paint. Let dry. 13. Spritz letters randomly over the Craft Sheet with Lettuce and Cranberry Color Wash. Rub a wet square of foam onto "high spots" and edges of letters, creating a distressed effect and dimension. • 14. Attach letters onto large canvas with Glossy Accents. • 15. Attach canvas boards accented with copper notions to larger canvas with Glossy Accents.

Tips and Techniques

1. To apply *Color Wash* onto *Cut 'n Dry Foam*, spray onto *Craft Sheet* and rub foam into it. You will have more control than trying to spray directly on the foam square.

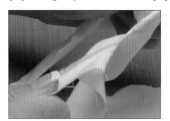

1. Rip or cut fabric strip.

3. Spritz fabric strip with *Color Wash*

4. Dry and heat set with *Heatit* Tool.

4. Attach strip to canvas with Fabri-Tac glue.

'Poppy and Maya' Canvas

by Jen Starr

Create interesting textures and distressed mottled textures with Color Wash techniques.

SIZE: 8" x 19"

MATERIALS: *Ranger Tim Holtz Adirondack Color Wash -* Espresso, Lettuce, Pesto • *Cut n' Dry Foam* • *Glossy Accents* • *Heatit* Craft Tool

SUPPLIES: Stretched canvas (8" x 10", 8" x 8") • Papers (*Scenic Route* Cerulean Jade Chestnut Stripe, Cerulean Chestnut Script) • *Scenic Route* Aqua Redmond Chipboard letters • White cardstock • *QuicKutz* die cuts (Sonja Font upper, lower) • Kosher Salt • Sandpaper • Paper towels • Hardware to connect canvases

INSTRUCTIONS:

1. Heavily spritz canvases with water and Espresso Color Wash. • 2. Throw kosher salt on wet Color Wash and water mixture. Let dry. • 3. Brush off excess kosher salt. See what a wonderful texture is created. • 4. Cut printed papers as follows: 8" circle: cut in half; 3" x 8" paper strip: tear one edge lengthwise; 3" x 3" square: cut diagonally to create corners. 5. Spritz Espresso Color Wash onto Craft Sheet and dip square of foam into it. Edge all papers using inked foam and let dry. 6. Glue all paper down. • 7. Lightly spritz full 12" x 12" sheet of White cardstock with water, followed by light mistings of Lettuce and Pesto Color Wash. Let dry or speed drying time with Heatit Tool. • 8. Use this paper for photo mats and for dies to spell "Remember" and "and". Glue in place. • 9. Choose chipboard letters to be used and lightly sand. Place onto Craft Sheet and spritz with Espresso Color Wash. Dab off any excess with paper towel. • 10. Attach letters to canvas with Glossy Accents. • 11. Attach canvas squares with hardware.

Adirondack Color Wash on Canvas

1. Spray canvas with water and *Color Wash.*

2. Sprinkle canvas with Kosher salt. Let dry.

3. Brush off salt.

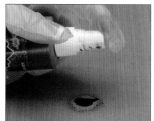

4. Spritz *Color Wash* onto craft sheet.

5. Dip *Cut n' Dry Foam* into *Color Wash.*

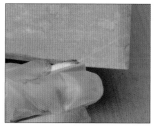

6. Ink edges of cardstock.

Adirondack Pigment Pens

Tips and Techniques

1. Impressions Fabric Sticker Canvas paper is very versatile due to the adhesive backing. Place on a card, scrapbook page or even a canvas bag.

2. Since the masking tape is not in and of itself archival, the Gel Medium provides archival properties to the masked tape surface on the clipboard.

3. Try other designs with the masking tape, laying out strips vertically, crisscrossing, or adding torn pieces randomly for different effects.

4. For hard-to-reach portions of the clipboard's metal clip, use a piece of felt directly in your hand to apply *Alcohol Ink*.

5. Add more water to *Adirondack Acrylics* if a very light wash of paint is desired.

6. *Decor it* is solvent-based pigment ink that will dry on all surfaces, porous and non-porous.

7. *Adirondack Pigment Pens* when wet are blendable, but when dry, are permanent, so this technique is perfect for anything wearable.

Treasured Tulips

by Robin Beam and Bonnie Egenton,
Masking Tape technique
by Claudine Hellmuth

Adirondack Pigment Pens are unique... they work on practically all surfaces! Create a pretty and useful clipboard for a "To Do List" with pens, Alcohol Inks, Acrylics & masking tape.

SIZE: 6" x 9"

MATERIALS: *Ranger Adirondack*: Alcohol Inks - Denim, Stream, Wild Plum; Alcohol Ink Applicator and Felt; Alcohol Ink Blending Solution; Pearlized Acrylics - Denim, Stream, Wild Plum; *Pigment Pens* - Bottle, Butterscotch, Caramel, Cranberry, Eggplant, Lettuce, Stream, Pesto, Red Pepper, Wild Plum • Black *Decor it* ink • *Cut n' Dry Foam* • *Inkssentials Non-Stick Craft Sheet* • *Cleansit* Stamp Cleaner • Water Mister

SUPPLIES: Rubber stamps (*Hero Arts* Treasure, Word Borders, Sketch Tulips, A Warm Hello) • *Niji* Waterbrush • 6" x 9" clipboard • Matte Gel Medium • Masking tape • 1½" paintbrush • Ribbon • Fibers • *Paper House Production* Blank Impressions Fabric Sticker • Scissors • Tulip *Post-it* note pads

INSTRUCTIONS:

Canvas Tulips: 1. Cut out a square of foam. Shake up and squeeze out some Decor it ink onto square.
2. Pat inked foam square onto Sketch Tulips stamp. Stamp in the center of the fabric. Ink stamp again 2 times and stamp on each side to create a line of tulips.
3. Ink and stamp "treasure" below the center set of tulips. • 4. Clean stamp with Cleansit Stamp Cleaner.
5. Scribble chosen color of Adirondack Pigment Pens

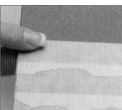

1. Wrap a clipboard with masking tape.

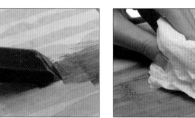

2. Brush on gel medium.

3. Paint surface with Denim Acrylic.

4. Dab ink with a wadded paper towel.

5. Scribble pens on a *Craft Sheet*.

6. Pick up ink with a waterbrush, then paint image.

on the Craft Sheet.
6. Pick up ink from the Craft Sheet with Waterbrush. Paint in image. The ink may stray outside of the lines of the stamped image for a watercolor effect.
7. Clean brush off between colors and continue painting in image.
8. Cut out fabric sticker to size. Use the sharp side of scissors to fray the edges of the fabric. Set aside.

Clipboard:
9. Wrap the clipboard with strips of masking tape horizontally. For a textured effect, gently rip masking tape and overlap pieces. • 10. Brush on a light coat of Gel Medium over the masking tape using the paintbrush. Let dry.
11. Using the Craft Sheet as a paint palette, squeeze out Denim Adirondack Acrylics and thin the paint with a spritz of water. Paint across the surface of the clipboard, painting carefully around metal clip. To remove some color, wad up a paper towel and remove in sections as desired. 12. Continue coloring in the same manner with Stream and Wild Plum Adirondack Acrylics. Let dry.
13. Lightly paint the clipboard edge with Stream and Denim Adirondack Acrylics. For a vibrant color, do not dilute with water. • 14. Using Alcohol Ink Applicator and Felt, place Adirondack Alcohol Inks in Stream, Denim and Wild Plum on felt. Stamp onto metal clip to colorize. Lighten with Adirondack Alcohol Ink Blending Solution as desired.

Assembly: 15. Attach Post-it Notes to top portion of clipboard.
16. Remove paper backing of stamped Impressions Fabric Sticker and mount to bottom portion of clipboard.
17. Add ribbons and fibers to loop on clip.

1. Color domino with *Pigment Pens*.

2. Smear ink with fingertip.

3. Stamp image onto domino.

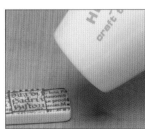
4. Heat set image on the domino.

5. Color background image with *Cut N' Dry Foam*.

Text Collage Domino Card
by Bonnie Egenton, technique by Tim Holtz

SIZE: 5" x 5¾"
MATERIALS: *Ranger Adirondack*: Pigment Pens - Butterscotch, Stream, Wild Plum; Dye Stamp Pads - Butterscotch, Stream, Wild Plum • Jet Black *Archival* Ink • *Cut n' Dry Foam* • *Heatit* Craft Tool • *Inkssentials Non-Stick Craft Sheet*
SUPPLIES: Rubber stamp (*Hampton Arts Limited Edition* Text Collage) • 3 small dominoes • *Wonder Tape* • Cardstock (White, Black, Butterscotch)

INSTRUCTIONS:
Background: 1. Stamp Text Collage with Jet Black ink on White cardstock.
2. Color image in using a small square of foam. Apply dye ink by gently rubbing area of image. Use one piece of foam for each ink color. • 3. Rip edges of image for a torn finish. • 4. Adhere to Black cardstock and layer to butterscotch cardstock. Set aside.
Dominoes: 5. Scribble Pigment Pens on domino. Start from lightest to darkest color; Butterscotch first, followed by Wild Plum and Stream. • 6. Blend and mute color with finger. Repeat with additional colors one at a time - Wild Plum and Stream. • 7. Ink Text Image in Jet Black ink and place stamp on work surface, ink side up. • 8. Determine placement of image on domino and carefully press onto stamp. Repeat with 2 more dominoes, using a different section of the image each time. • 9. Attach dominos with Wonder Tape to front of card, lining up with stamped image.

Tips and Techniques

1. *Adirondack Pigment Pens* are blendable when wet, permanent when dry.

2. When tearing paper, always tear towards you to get the most textured look from the paper.

3. When stamping dominoes or other small surfaces, always place the stamp on the work surface stamp side up and press the item to be stamped down into the stamp to assure exact placement. Lift the inked item straight up off of the stamp for a crisp image every time.

4. Make a card with a domino pin as a gift – attach a pin back and adhere to front of card with hook and loop tape so the pin can be removed.

5. Create a domino card with spot coloring. Stamp image in Jet Black *Archival Ink* on White card. Color domino with *Pigment Pens* and stamp same image. The domino becomes the spotlight and pops off of the Black and White card.

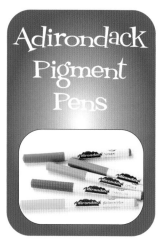

Adirondack Pigment Pens

1. Color back of image with a *Pigment Pen*.

2. Add jewels with *Adirondack Acrylics*.

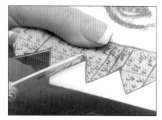

3. Cut out card.

4. Line cardstock with a Gold *Posh Accent Pen*.

5. Adhere vellum to cardstock.

The Princess Card

by Bonnie Egenton, technique by Tim Holtz

SIZE: 5½" x 7"

MATERIALS: *Ranger* Jet Black *Archival* Ink pad • *Adirondack*: Butterscotch Acrylics; *Pigment Pens* - Butterscotch, Caramel, Ginger, Latte, Lettuce, Meadow, Red Pepper, Stonewashed • Gold *Posh Accent Pen* • Worn Lipstick *Tim Holtz Distress* Ink pad • *Cut n' Dry Foam* • *Heatit* Craft Tool • *Non-Stick Craft Sheet*

SUPPLIES: Rubber stamps (*Stampers Anonymous* Ledger Border, West Indies Corner; *Hampton Arts Limited Edition* Large Face) • Vellum paper • Cardstock (White, Black) • Ribbon • 1/16" hole punch • Brad • Vellum adhesive • Glue stick

INSTRUCTIONS:

1. Stamp Face with Jet Black ink on vellum. Let dry. • 2. Stamp West Indies Corner with Jet Black ink, lining up to frame the Face image. Let dry. • 3. Stamp Ledger Border as a "crown" above the Face image with Jet Black ink. Let dry. • 4. On the reverse side of the vellum, color images using Pigment Pens. Color areas in and using finger, pull ink to uninked area, creating a "watercolor" type of effect. • 5. To make Pigment Pens permanent on the vellum, heat with the Heatit Tool. • 6. Using a piece of foam, ink cheeks on face image lightly with Worn Lipstick Distress Ink. • 7. Adhere vellum to White cardstock and trim around image on three sides. • 8. On fourth side, tear White cardstock. Tear vellum so that it slightly overlaps the White cardstock. • 9. Punch hole on left side of image and use a brad to attach ribbon. • 10. Attach image to Black card. • 11. Edge Black card with Gold pen. • 12. Create "jewels" on crown by placing dots of Butterscotch Acrylics. Let dry.

Tips and Techniques

1. When tearing paper, always tear towards you to get the most textured look from the paper. If you want a finer tear with less texture, tear away from you.

2. *Adirondack Pigment Pens* are water-based pigments that are blendable when wet, but become permanent when heat set or air dry.

3. *Adirondack Pigment Pens* work on both porous and non-porous surfaces.

4. Use on vellum paper, *Gloss Paper*, fabric, dominoes, acetate, shrink plastic, wood and metal.

Memory Glass

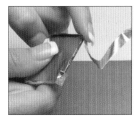

1. Apply *Adirondack Acrylics* to *Memory Glass*.

2. Sandwich ink with second piece of glass and squeeze together.

3. Wrap the edges of pieces of glass with foil tape.

Hi! Memory Glass Tile Pins and Card
by Rebecca Peck

SIZE: 4¼" x 5½"

MATERIALS: *Ranger Memory Glass* - Six 1½" Squares • Aluminum *Memory Foil Tape* • *Adirondack*: Acrylics - Lettuce, Stream, Wild Plum; Dye Stamp Pad - Lettuce, Stream, Wild Plum • Silver *Posh Accent* Pen • *Inkssentials Non-Stick Craft Sheet* • 3½" x 5½" *Gloss Paper* • *Cut n' Dry Foam* • *Paper Creaser*/bone folder)

SUPPLIES: Rub-on letters • Teal cardstock (2 x 5½"; 5½" x 8½") • Double-stick tape • Craft knife • Pin backs

INSTRUCTIONS:

1. Place a piece of Memory Glass on the Craft Sheet. • 2. Randomly apply drops of the Acrylics to the glass, being careful not to put them too close together. • 3. Gently lay another piece of Memory Glass on top of the first one, and apply light pressure to get the paint to fill in the gaps on the glass. Some paint will ooze out the sides, but this will easily scrape off the sides with a craft knife once the piece is dry. • 4. Repeat this process for the other two tiles, and then set the pieces aside to dry for 24 hours. • 5. Once the pieces are dry, wrap the edges with the foil tape. • 6. Apply the rub-on letters. • 7. Score and fold the 5½" x 8½" piece of Teal cardstock to make a 4¼" x 5½" card. • 8. Randomly apply Lettuce, Wild Plum and Stream inks to the glossy cardstock using a squares of foam. • 9. Edge the small piece of Teal cardstock and the glossy cardstock with Posh Accent Pen and assemble the card with double-stick tape or adhesive of choice. • 10. To create jewelry, rather than placing on a card, attach a pin back to it and it's ready to wear. Better yet, attach the pin back to the Memory Glass and attach to a card - wearable art and a card in one.

It is easy to personalize *Memory Glass* with a rub-on name, initials or a cheerful message.

Tips and Techniques

1. To apply *Memory Foil Tape*, remove just a small amount of the paper backing from the tape. You never want to remove the entire length of backing, because the foil will curl up into a ball. Trust us on this.

2. Center the tape on the bottom, center portion of the glass on the center of the tape, adhesive side up. Working on the *Craft Sheet* is best.

3. "Walk" the glass along the tape, removing the paper backing as you go. If, as you go along, you are no longer centered with the glass, just lift it off and center again.

4. When you get to the end, overlap the foil a little bit. Cut.

5. With your fingers, press down the four sides of the tape, using your finger and thumb to push down on each side of the glass.

6. For the corners, use a *Paper Creaser* (bone folder) and press down to one side or the other to "miter" the corners. Use the bone creaser to burnish the foil, removing any wrinkles. Remember not to push too hard, as it is glass.

Memory Glass

A BeaDazzling Shaker
by Debbie Tlach

SIZE: 2" x 2"

MATERIALS: *Ranger* Two 2" squares of Memory Glass, *Popit! Shapes* Letters • *BeaDazzles* Purple Rain

SUPPLIES: *Wonder Tape* • Small flat container

INSTRUCTIONS:
1. Adhere Popit! Shapes letters L, O, V, E onto a square of glass. • 2. Adhere a second square of glass onto the letters. • 3. Apply Wonder Tape along 3 sides covering the gap between the glass. • 4. Pour BeaDazzles into the channel between the glass pieces. • 5. Tape the remaining side of the glass, allowing for ¼" overlap of tape. • 6. Carefully remove the red protective covering from the tape and gently press the extra ¼" of tape around the edge overlapping and sealing the edges. • 7. Pour BeaDazzles into the flat container and dip the tape-covered sides into the container, coating all the sides. Press gently to make sure the BeaDazzles are adhered well. • 8. Shake the frame to coat the tape on the inside.

BeaDazzles
Shake
and
Move
Inside
the Glass

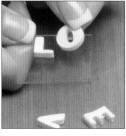

1. Adhere letters to *Memory Glass*.

2. Remove letter backing & place glass over the top.

3. Adhere *Wonder Tape* to 3 sides of the glass.

4. Pour *BeaDazzles* in between glass pieces. Seal with foil.

5. Pour *BeaDazzles* onto a plate, remove tape backing & dip.

1. Clean *Memory Glass* with *Blending Solution.*

2. Apply *Alcohol Ink* to glass with an applicator.

3. Stamp an image onto glass.

4. Layer glass pieces on top of each other.

5. Place a white piece of paper behind glass.

6. Wrap the edges of glass with foil tape.

Color Glass with Alcohol Inks

Angel Card
by Michele Charles

Create a beautiful card with glowing colors of Alcohol Ink.

SIZE: 4" x 4"

MATERIALS: *Ranger Adirondack* Alcohol inks - Stream, Butterscotch, Wild Plum • Gold *Metallic Mixative* ink • *Glossy Accents* • Jet Black *Archival* ink • *Memory Glass* 2 pieces of 2" x 2"; 2 pieces of $1\frac{1}{2}$" x $1\frac{1}{2}$"

SUPPLIES: Rubber stamps (*Magenta* Ironwork Background; *Stampers Anonymous* Face) • *Design Originals - Tim Holtz Aqua distressables cardstock* • Scallop foil tape

INSTRUCTIONS:

Begin: 1. Cut cardstock to 4" x 8". Fold to 4" x 4". Stamp background in Jet Black ink.

Background - Glass Square: 2. Apply Alcohol and Metallic Ink onto surface of 2" x 2" glass piece. Stamp the opposite side with text stamp in black ink. Cut a 2" x 2" white piece of paper and place on back. Place a second piece of 2" x 2" glass on top. Wrap foil tape around outside edge.

Top Glass Square: 3. Apply Alcohol and Metallic Ink to surface of $1\frac{1}{2}$" x $1\frac{1}{2}$" glass piece. Stamp angel image on second piece of glass in Black. Place both inked sides of glass together (stamped image will be reversed). Cut a $1\frac{1}{2}$" x $1\frac{1}{2}$" piece of White paper and place behind glass. Wrap foil tape around outside edge.

Assembly: 4. Adhere small piece of glass to top of larger glass piece with Glossy Accents. Adhere glass decoration to center of card with Glossy Accents.

Embossing Powders

Ranger Embossing Powders Tips and Techniques

Ranger offers a large variety of Embossing Powders, each with specific features to create exactly the look you want on all of your papercrafting projects. Try using the same stamped image on white cardstock with different powders and discover the numerous looks you can achieve. Ink the stamp with Clear Embossing Ink and see the difference when you ink the same image with black or any other color Pigment Ink but with exactly the same Embossing Powder. Stamp on Black cardstock to see how the same Embossing Powders create a very different effect.

Ranger was the first to bring heat embossing to rubber stampers in 1980 with Clear Embossing Powder. Now *Ranger* has over 100 powders to choose from ranging in finishes from shiny, metallic, puffy, textured, antiqued, pearlized and glitzy. All of *Ranger's* Embossing Powders are non-toxic and acid free for use in Scrapbooking Albums and Photo Journals.

Types of Embossing Powders:

Ranger Original Embossing Powders – contains a variety of Embossing Powders that create raised metallic, sparkly and opaque finishes. This also includes fun, "retro" colors such as Lemon Yellow, Mint Green, Candy Pink and Orange Sherbet.

Ultra Thick Embossing Enamel (UTEE) - is a specially formulated, large particle Embossing Powder. Use the *Heatit* Tool to produce an extra-thick embossed image or melt *UTEE* in the *Melting Pot*. Pour into molds to create 3-D artifacts or dip to coat a variety of objects for one-of-a-kind art and jewelry. Comes in a variety of colors and sized jars, including Clear, Black, White, Platinum, Bronze, Interference Blue, Gold, Pearl and Red Hot.

UTEE Brightz - These *Ultra Thick Embossing Enamels* have an opaque, pearlescent quality and come in breathtakingly vibrant colors. They'll add extra shimmer and pizazz to all your *Melt Art* and embossing projects. Discover the floral beauty of Fuchsia, Tiger Lily, Sunflower, Green Zinnia, Blue Iris and Violet.

Super Fine Detail Embossing Powder – Fine Embossing Powders ideal for very detailed stamp images.

Embossing Pearls - Pearlized, Interference Embossing Powders for subtle, pearl elegance on light papers, and more dramatic pearlized effects on dark papers.

Adirondack Embossing Powder – Semi-matte finish that coordinates beautifully with the rest of the *Adirondack* product line. Their unique quality allows for beautiful, speckled mixtures of color ideal for autumn and vintage images.

Distress Powder –Specifically designed to match *Distress Ink* colors, these matte, textured Embossing Powders have a special property. After embossing, rub off the special release crystals to create a weathered, worn effect.

Ancient Golds Embossing Powder – are metallic golds in a variety of finishes from bright to antique. Also included are clear-based Embossing Powders with encrusted finishes for a golden, glittery effect.

Embossing Antiquities – Semi-matte and matte Embossing Powder with an all-over even textured effect that achieves the look of faux stone. Some have a mixture of metallic in it for added sheen.

Embossing Puffs – Create a warm, fuzzy look that puffs when heated for surface dimension. Perfect for embossing teddy bear or other animal images.

Embossing Glitter – Glitter you can emboss. It's in a clear base to let the ink color and paper underneath show through.

Embossing Tinsel – Show glitz and glamour with glitter in an opaque or pearl embossing powder base. Try it on white or light cardstock or pile on the glitz on dark cardstock. Bridal Tinsel is the perfect mix of color for any wedding card or invitation.

Tips When Embossing:

Embossing Powders can be used over any type of water-based ink including dye, pigment and embossing inks. When working with dye ink, move quickly since dye ink is fast-drying.

To stamp with embossing ink, begin by inking your stamp with *Emboss it*, *Big & Bossy* Clear, *Big & Bossy* Two-Tone, *Big & Bossy* Tinted, or *Distress* Embossing Ink. Stamp image onto matte or *Gloss Paper*.

Use scrap paper under your stamped image when pouring embossing powder. Remove excess powder by sliding it off the card surface onto the scrap paper. Tap the back of the image with your finger to release additional excess powder that doesn't stick to the embossing ink. Be sure to return the excess embossing powder on the scrap paper back to the jar for the next use – no waste.

If any stray embossing powder is still on the paper, use a small paintbrush to whisk it off of the surface – otherwise it will melt onto the paper when heat embossed.

Remember that Clear Embossing Ink will not affect the color of the embossing powder. Tinted inks might affect the color of the embossing powder depending upon how clear or light the base of the embossing powder is. For instance, if the tinted ink has a blue base, and the embossing powder has a clear base, the finished embossing may appear to have a blue tint.

Use the *Ranger Inkssentials Craft Sheet* to protect your work surface when heat embossing your stamped image.

Embossing powders can be melted with the *Heatit* Tool or in the *Melting Pot*.

When using the *Heatit* Tool, first warm it up for a few seconds before aiming at the paper to

Ranger Embossing Powder

Ultra Thick Embossing Enamel

Super Fine Detail Embossing Powder

emboss. Hold the *Heatit* Tool a few inches away from the paper surface and heat evenly. As soon as you see the embossing change – whether raised, metallic, glitter, or matte, the heating is completed.

When using *UTEE*, slowly bring the *Heatit* Tool down to the paper surface from several inches above to warm the *UTEE* and help it melt more easily.

When using most pigment ink on glossy paper, you must use embossing powder and heat emboss or the pigment ink will never dry on this non-porous surface.

Don't be afraid to mix and match embossing powders to create your own recipes/combinations for added fun. Check out *Ranger*'s Embossing Powders Recipe Book for ideas.

Embossing powders can be used on paper, paper mache, wood, and clay.

Embossing Powders Primer Samples

Samples pictured on page 48 by Bonnie Egenton

Make samples by trying different types of Embossing Powder to create varied effects. See how using Super Fine Detail, regular, and Ultra Thick can give distinctively different outcomes on paper.
MATERIALS: Ranger (Black *Super Fine Detail* Embossing Powder • Black Embossing Powder • *Ultra Thick Embossing Enamel/UTEE* • *Big & Bossy* Clear Embossing Pad • White *Gloss Paper* • *Heatit* Craft Tool • Inkssentials Non-Stick Craft Sheet)
SUPPLIES: Rubber stamp (*Just for Fun* Tree in Winter)
INSTRUCTIONS: 1. Ink up stamp with Embossing Ink and stamp image on White Gloss paper. Repeat 2 times on additional pieces of White Gloss paper. • Shake Black Super Fine Detail Embossing Powder over first stamped image and tap off excess onto scrap paper. Return excess powder to jar. • 3. Emboss additional images with Black Embossing Powder and Black UTEE. 4. On Craft Sheet, emboss each image with Heat it Tool until melted.

Tips and Techniques

1. Notice on page 48 how each embossing powder created different results with the same stamped image. Regular embossing powder creates a slightly heavier, less detailed result.

2. *Ultra Thick Embossing Enamel* creates a very thick and less defined tree that actually looks like it could be a plant at the bottom of the sea.

3. *Super Fine Detail* Powder shows the fine and delicate detail of the tree branches.

1. Sprinkle Silver Embossing Powder over stamped image.

2. Emboss with *HeatIt* Tool.

3. Lay vellum onto cardstock and trim.

4. Punch two holes at top of the card.

5. Weave ribbon through the holes.

Tips and Techniques

1. Be careful when embossing with vellum to not overemboss and burn the paper.

2. The *Heatit* Tool is wonderful to use because it is more diffused air, but it does get as hot

Silver Pearlized Wedding Card

by Robin Beam

Some embossing powders will look different depending on the ink that is beneath it. Embossing Pearls, such as the Silver Pearl used for this wonderful wedding card, looks like a totally different powder because of the color of the ink beneath it.
SIZE: 6¼" x 6¼"
MATERIALS: *Ranger* Silver *Embossing Pearls* • Platinum *Color it* Pigment Ink Stamp Pad • *Big & Bossy* Clear Embossing Pad • *Heatit* Craft Tool • Inkssentials Non-Stick *Craft Sheet*
SUPPLIES: Rubber stamps (*Another Stamp Company* Bride & Groom, Small Cake Topper; *Hero Arts* Cherish) • Vellum • Cardstock (White, Silver) • Small hole punch • Ribbon
INSTRUCTIONS:
1. Cut White cardstock 5¾" x 5¾". • 2. Ink Small Cake Topper stamp with Clear Embossing Ink. • 3. On left side of White cardstock, stamp image multiple times. • 4. Sprinkle on Silver Embossing Pearls. Shake off excess and return to jar. • 5. Heat emboss with Heatit Tool over the Craft Sheet. • 6. Cut vellum 4¼" x 5¾". • 7. Ink Bride & Groom image with Platinum pigment ink. Stamp image on center vellum. Ink and stamp "cherish" image with Platinum ink above bride and groom image. • 8. Heat emboss with Silver Embossing Pearls. • 9. Cut Silver cardstock slightly larger than the vellum. • 10. Overlay vellum to White cardstock, centering on Silver cardstock. Punch two holes and weave through ribbon.

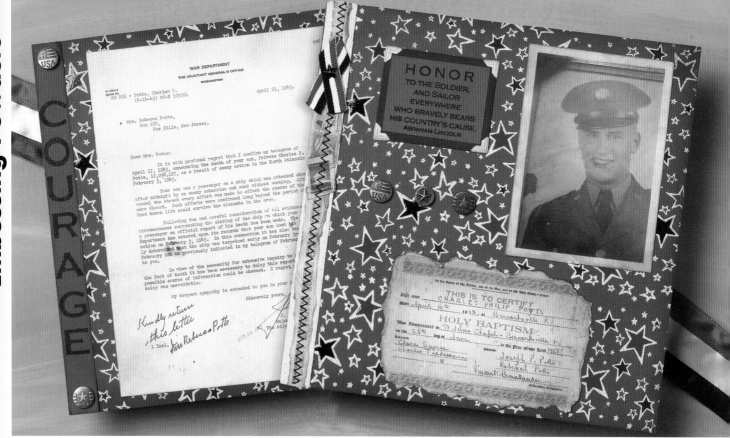

'Honor and Courage' Embossed Scrapbook Page

by Bonnie Egenton

Create your own customized background papers for scrapbook pages with stamps and Embossing Powder to achieve the exact look you want.

SIZE: 12" x 12"

MATERIALS: Ranger *Embossing Antiquities* - Weathered White, Cobalt • *Big & Bossy* Clear Embossing Pad • *Heatit* Craft Tool • *Inkssentials Non-Stick Craft Sheet* • *Adirondack* Denim Pigment Pen • *Glossy Accents* • *Tim Holtz Distress* Ink pads - Antique Linen, Tea Dye, Walnut Stain • *Cut n' Dry Foam*

SUPPLIES: Rubber stamps (*Postmodern Design* Honor; *DeNami Design* Star Outline; *Magnetic Poetry* Traditional Alphabet) • 12" x 12" cardstock (3 Red, 1 Blue) • White photo corners • Glue stick • Stitched border • Metal Art Military Emblems • Copies of photos on photo paper • Copies of baptism and War Department documents

INSTRUCTIONS:
1. Ink up Honor stamp with embossing ink. Stamp image on small piece of Red cardstock and stamp "COURAGE" with embossing ink on 1" x 12" Red strip.
2. Shake Cobalt Embossing Antiquities Powder over stamped words. Tap off excess onto scrap paper and return to jar. • 3. Place on Craft Sheet and emboss images with the Heatit Tool until melted. • 4. Mat Honor image with Blue cardstock and attach White photo corners. Set aside both embossed images. • 5. Stamp two 12" x 12" Red cardstocks with Stars stamp inked with embossing ink. • 6. Shake Weathered White Embossing Antiquities Powder over stars and tap off excess onto scrap paper and emboss. • 7. Pick out some stars to spot color with Denim Adirondack Pigment Pen. • 8. Accent some of the Denim stars with Glossy Accents. Begin by tracing inside the embossing line of the star and fill in. Repeat process with some of the red stars. • 9. Let dry to a dimensional clear gloss. • 10. Ink edges of the Honor and Courage stamped pieces, both 12" x 12" embossed pages, the photo, Baptism and War Department documents with Antique Linen, Tea Dye, and Walnut Ink Distress Inks by inking small pieces of foam and rubbing along the edges to create a soft, vintage effect. • 11. Assemble pages with photo, documents and stamped images. Carefully press Metal Art Military Emblems through the papers and lightly hammer on the reverse side of pages.
12. Add Stitched Borders to outside of pages.

Tips and Techniques

1. *Embossing Antiquities* give a textured, matte effect. These Embossing Powders are ideal for a more subtle, aged look to a page or card.

2. *Glossy Accents* is a 3-dimensional, clear gloss medium that can accent and brighten a page or card. Using *Glossy Accents* on the stars provides a dimension and pop to an otherwise flat and level surface. Practice on scrap paper first, creating a flow and removing any air bubbles.

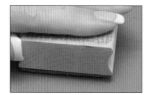

1. Stamp image with embossing ink.

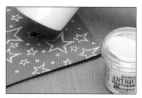

2. Emboss with *Heatit* tool.

3. Color random stars with Denim *Pigment Pen.*

4. Spot embellish with *Glossy Accents.*

5. Ink the edges of pages to add a distressed look.

6. Distress the edges of "Honor" journal box.